The Handmaiden's HANDBOOK

*A Spiritual Guide for Women
Who Serve Women Leaders
God's Way*

Volume One
"A Divine Assignment"

Denise M. Carlie

Unless otherwise indicated, all Scripture quotations and adaptions are taken from the **King James Version** of the Bible.

All Scriptures marked **AMP** are taken from the **Amplified Bible**. Copyright© 2015 by The Lockman Foundation, La Habra, CA 90631. All rights reserved.

All Scriptures marked **AMPC** are taken from the **Amplified Bible**. Copyright© 1954, 1958, 1962, 1964, 1965, 1987 by The Lockman Foundation.

All Scriptures marked **NASB** are taken from the **New American Standard Bible**˚. Copyright © 1960, 1962, 1963, 1968, 1971, 1972, 1973, 1975, 1977, 1995 by The Lockman Foundation. Used by permission.

All Scriptures marked **CEV** are taken from the **Contemporary English Version**˚. Copyright© 1995 American Bible Society. All rights reserved.

All Scriptures marked **TLV** are taken from the **Tree of Life Version of the Bible**. Copyright© 2015 by The Messianic Jewish Family Bible Society.

All Scriptures marked **MSG** are taken from **The Message**. Copyright© 1993, 1994, 1995, 1996, 2000, 2001, 2002. Used by the permission of NavPress Publishing Group.

All Scriptures marked **NIV** are taken from **THE HOLY BIBLE, NEW INTERNATIONAL VERSION**˚, **NIV**˚. Copyright © 1973, 1978, 1984, 2011 by Biblica, Inc.˚ Used by permission. All rights reserved worldwide.

All Scriptures marked **NKJV** are taken from the **New King James Version**˚. Copyright© 1982 by Thomas Nelson. Used by permission. All rights reserved.

All Scriptures marked **TLB** are taken from **The Living Bible**. Copyright© 1971 by Tyndale House Foundation. Used by permission of Tyndale House Publishers Inc., Carol Stream, Illinois 60188. All rights reserved.

All Scriptures marked **NLT** are taken from the **Holy Bible, New Living Translation**. Copyright© 1996, 2004, 2015 by Tyndale House Foundation. Used by permission of Tyndale House Publishers, Inc., Carol Stream, Illinois 60188. All rights reserved.

All Scriptures marked **The VOICE** are taken from **The Voice Bible**. Copyright© 2012 Thomas Nelson, Inc. The Voice™ Translation© 2012 Ecclesia Bible Society. All rights reserved.

All Scriptures marked **GNT** are taken from the **Good News Translation**˚ (Today's English Version, Second Edition). Copyright© 1992 American Bible Society. All rights reserved.

All Scriptures marked **CEB** are taken from the **Common English Bible**. Copyright 2011 by the Common English Bible. All rights reserved. Used by permission.

All Scriptures marked **TPT** are taken from **The Passion Translation**˚. Copyright© 2017 by Passion & Fire Ministries, Inc. Used by permission. All rights reserved. www.ThePassionTranslation.com

The Handmaiden's Handbook: A Spiritual Guide for Women Who Serve Women Leaders God's Way Volume One "A Divine Assignment"
by Denise M. Carlie

ISBN: 978-0-578-84171-7
LCCN: 2021900938

Published by Denise M. Carlie

P. O. Box 1073

North Riverside, IL 60546 All rights reserved.

Contents and cover may not be reproduced in whole or in part in any form without the express written consent of the author or publisher.

Manifesting the heart of my King through the written word.

"The path to promotion and prominence comes by having the heart of a bond-slave who serves everyone. For even the Son of Man did not come expecting to be served by everyone, but to serve everyone, and to give his life as the ransom price in exchange for the salvation of many."

Jesus Christ
Mark 10:44–45 (TPT)

A Word from the Lord for Modern-day Handmaidens

"Today, I have called you to this place of greatness. This is a place that doesn't look like what it really is to the natural eye. It looks like a demeaning place; a place of low value and low worth. But know, My handmaiden, that when you bow, it is a posture of humility. To bend to serve another honors them and places you in a position to be exalted by Me. It is your willingness to lay aside your own agenda in the service of another that is precious in My sight. Remember that I am the God that looks at the heart and not at the outward appearance of man. My standard for greatness is different than the standard of the world in which you live. As you continue to serve another, know that I am building a solid structure within you. Your character will be strong enough to handle the weight of the things that I will allow you to witness and participate in because of your association. Be not afraid to lay aside your aspirations so another can go forward. Be not afraid to "walk in the shadows of another," for it is in these shadows that you will find Me…and discover your true self."

Table of Contents

Introduction	ix
1. The Evolution of Women Serving Women	1
2. Heaven Has an Agenda	11
3. God Needs Women Too!	21
4. Handpicked by God	43
5. A Divine Assignment	57
6. No Time for Fear	65
7. Cultivating a Servant's Heart	79
8. Cultivating Your Leader's Heart	101
The Handmaiden's Prayer	119
Special Thanks!	121
About the Book	123
Endnotes	125
About the Author	129
Contact the Author	129

Introduction

Everyone strives to achieve their *own* dreams…but very few are willing and able to lay those dreams aside to help *someone else* achieve theirs. There is an old saying, *"Many are called, but few are chosen."* Those that have been chosen to lead deserve to be served with honor for the sacrifice that they make, and those who have been called to help them are expected to do it competently, wholeheartedly, and with excellence. Some may consider serving another person to be demeaning and thankless…while others may envy it, depending upon the status of the one being served.

If you are reading this book, it's probably because you are either already serving a leader or may have been asked to do so. Your leader is probably a woman, which is the focus of this book. (But if your leader happens to be a man, *keep reading*, because the principles shared are universal, no matter the gender of the leader.) Either way, the most important thing you need to know is that you have been chosen by God to serve your leader, and this is a very high honor that shouldn't be taken lightly.

Think about it. Of all the people your leader may know, have talked to, or considered, they selected *you*…and it's up to you to serve them in such a spirit of excellence that you set a standard that others want to emulate. Not only are you able to do it, but you are able to do it at the highest level!

I am the Executive Personal Assistant to an awesome woman who, along with her husband, leads a ministry that has the potential to reach over 800 million households worldwide. I started supporting her by becoming the Women's Ministry Director for our church. It was a natural progression that took me from helping her part-time to becoming her full-time support staff. The transition was a smooth one, because my heart toward her and toward what I believed that God had called me to do never changed. It has always been my desire to serve my first lady, my boss, my sister in Christ, and my friend in any way I can. Anyone who knows me knows this to be true.

It was, however, never my plan to work for my first lady in *this* capacity. As a matter of fact, when I first met her, I was working full-time and making really good money. I served her in our women's ministry for more than five years before this opportunity came about, and I was still serving her when my employer moved to another state, leaving me without a job. My journey to becoming her personal assistant happened supernaturally. Why do I say it happened supernaturally? Because when I looked back over how it all came about, I could see the hand of God orchestrating it every step of the way…but I had a part to play. I had to use my FAITH!

I was always willing to do whatever my first lady asked me to, because it helped me to fill my time since I wasn't working…or so I thought. I found myself moving from just overseeing women's ministry events to handling personal matters for her as well. What I didn't realize was that I was being prepared for promotion without doing anything other than serving her with a pure heart. I wasn't looking for anything from her…in fact, I was looking to go back to work in corporate America where I came from! **Proverbs 16:9 (KJV)** says, "*A man's heart deviseth his way, but* *the Lord directeth his steps."* Another translation says it like this: *"People may make plans in their minds, but the Lord decides what they will do." **(NCT)*** God had decided what I was going to do.

One day, while I was sitting at my computer completing my weekly unemployment forms, I received a call out of the blue from my first lady, asking me if I would like to be her Executive Personal Assistant. I didn't hesitate. I didn't even think about it...I just said, *"Yes."* Not because I was unemployed and needed a job, but because *my heart had already stepped into the role long before she asked.* We were both very excited about the possibilities of what we would be able to accomplish, now that she had full-time help. There was just one catch. We needed the final approval of the man of God—our pastor—and he was out of the country on the mission field for two weeks!

Anyone who knows our pastor knows that he doesn't make decisions quickly or lightly, he doesn't do anything without hearing from God first, and he won't allow *anyone* to pressure him into deciding something apart from God's approval. We prayed in agreement, believing that this was right, and that God would finish what He started. I released it to the Lord in my heart, standing on **Proverbs 21:1**, *"The king's heart is like a stream of water directed by the LORD; he guides it wherever he pleases."* **(NLT)**

As I mentioned, when this opportunity came along, I was out of work and had been actively looking for employment. In my search, I came across a position with a law firm that I had worked very closely with at my former job. It was a prestigious firm, and I had always wanted to work for them but could never get in. I had even reached out to them for possible employment when we were first notified that my employer was relocating, but had no success. This firm must have been a great place to work, because their employees never left and open opportunities were extremely rare. I had also heard that they treated their employees very well. When I saw that they had a management position open, I immediately jumped on it.

Months went by and I didn't hear anything, leading me to assume that the law firm had hired someone else. But right after I said yes to my first lady—the *very same week*—I got a call from this law firm, wanting me to come in for an interview! I convinced myself that since my pastor was still out of the country, I didn't *officially* have a job, so I scheduled the interview.

After jumping through all the hoops and doing all the twirls, I got a call informing me that I didn't get the position, even though I was qualified for it. Instead, they wanted to offer me a lower senior position. The same prestigious company, great salary, benefits galore…and it was being handed to me with no questions asked other than when could I start. I now had a serious dilemma.

I asked the recruiter if I could have a few days to decide, and they granted my request. My rational mind reminded me that I was unemployed, my bills were due, and I needed an income right now! The voice of reason said that the position offered to me by my first lady really didn't exist…and wouldn't until our pastor gave his approval. It told me that the law firm position was a sure thing; I could take it immediately and be back to work with a steady income in a few days. I was torn. I didn't want to be selfish, knowing that my family was in need, but my heart was telling me that I had committed to something that was greater than what I could see.

I talked it over with my husband, hoping he would make the decision for me and tell me sternly that we needed the money and

Introduction

I should take the position with the law firm. He didn't. Instead, he told me that the decision was mine to make and then assured me that he was with me, no matter what I decided. Well that didn't help! I still had a decision to make.

That same week, my daughter and her family came in from out of town for a visit. I shared the situation with them. We all gathered in a circle in our living room and prayed as a family, asking God to give me wisdom to make the right decision.

Well, I guess you can tell by my opening sentence what I decided. I called the law firm back, thanked them for their consideration, and turned down their offer. I walked away from a well-paying job with a very prestigious law firm...and *I have never regretted my decision for even one day.* I know that I am doing something very important that has eternal implications. I am inside the will of God, doing what I have been called to do... providing support to another woman who has been called by God to a position of leadership.

Why this book?

What led me to write this book is that while travelling with my first lady to various churches and hosting events at our own church, I've had the opportunity to observe and interact with many women who do what I do. While some appeared to serve their leader well, I noticed that in far too many instances, the service being provided was lacking and not up to the standard of excellence that their leaders deserve and God expects. (This is not an indictment...merely an observation.) I concluded that for the most part, these women had been placed in their position without the benefit of training and mentoring. They were asked (and they accepted) without understanding the spiritual magnitude of their role, which should impact how they perform their duties practically. Please understand: *My goal is not to condemn anyone but to prayerfully raise an awareness and the standard of this very important position.* My desire is to bring a spirit of holiness, humility, and honor to what we are called to do. I also want to share the spiritual and natural wisdom I've learned over the years while serving my first lady.

The foundation for all that is written in this handbook is the Holy Bible. It governs *how I live*, and *the way I serve*. Therefore, I have chosen to use characters, situations, and Scriptures from the Holy Bible to help me highlight the principles focused on in this work. This is the first in a series of three handbooks. The second book will focus on character development, specifically key characteristics that are necessary to fulfill this high calling. Some of the topics that will be covered are *integrity, honor, humility, faithfulness,* and *serving in excellence*. The third book will be more hands on, with a focus on practical application. It will be filled with wisdom nuggets for serving, such as *discretion and confidentiality, the importance of being seen and not heard, being led by the Spirit concerning the proper attire, not trying to upstage your leader,* and much more!

I call this a "handbook" because it is my prayer that you will refer to it again and again, especially when outside forces and internal voices try to make you believe that what you do is not important. Whether you're a "seasoned servant" or a "newbie," I prophesy that you will receive an impartation of the significance of your assignment, and that it will cause a passion to be ignited in your heart that will propel you to perform at such a high level of service that even your leaders will stand up and take notice!

God has chosen you as His Handmaiden to serve His Leader!

CHAPTER 1

The Evolution of Women Serving Women

※⁕※

"But Ruth said, 'Don't force me to leave you; don't make me go home. Where you go, I go; and where you live, I'll live. Your people are my people, your God is my god; where you die, I'll die and that's where I'll be buried, so help me God—not even death itself is going to come between us!' When Naomi saw that Ruth had her heart set on going with her, she gave in."

(Ruth 1:16-18 MSG)

NAOMI had decided that there was nothing keeping her in Moab. Although she had called it home for many years, she was still a foreigner, and it was time for her to return to the land of her fathers. The loss of her husband and two sons had become a shroud of grief over her, so heavy that she didn't have the strength or will to get out from under it. She was convinced that her last glimmer of hope was about to go out, and she couldn't see any other solution but to send her two daughters-in-law back to their families. Moab was their home; and although her heart was breaking, she believed that it was best for them. They were void of spiritual covering, and there was no one left to provide for or protect them. One of them had already heeded her urging and was on her journey home.

The other daughter, Ruth, had decided to stay with her. Naomi couldn't comprehend why Ruth was willing to do the very same thing that she had done many years earlier—leave her home country, sojourn to a foreign land that she knew nothing about, and make it her home. Naomi had nothing to offer or promise Ruth, yet she was still willing to lay down her life and go with her. Naomi desperately tried to convince Ruth to go home to her family—but to no avail. She would eventually concede, moved by Ruth's vow to go wherever she went, to live in her land and among her people, to serve her God, and even die where she died. Ruth's decision to stay with Naomi meant more than either of them would ever know.

Ruth loved her husband, who was Naomi's son. She also loved Naomi and didn't want to leave her alone. Ruth considered Naomi to be more than just her mother-in-law. They were two very different women who had been brought together and stayed together under what appeared to be impossible circumstances. Ruth was a Moabite, and Naomi was a Hebrew. Ruth was young, and Naomi was seasoned. Ruth was the student, and Naomi was her teacher. So very different…yet so much alike. They both loved Naomi's son. They both loved Naomi's God. The vow that Ruth made to Naomi was not made from a place of emotion or fear, but from a place of deep faith that she learned by example as she watched Naomi serve her God. Naomi had made an indelible mark on Ruth that could not be erased.

Naomi's grief over the loss of her husband and two sons caused her to misjudge her God, but her continued commitment to Him was demonstrated in her training of Ruth, which ultimately set them up to live together in prosperity and abundance for the rest of their lives.

Naomi was no common, ordinary woman. She was a leader and an influencer. A footnote in an online commentary said that the reason the entire town came out to greet her when she returned home was because her husband may have held a place of prominence. An entire town is not going to come out for just anyone. If her husband was considered a prominent leader, then by association, she was too. Naomi and Ruth had no knowledge of the impact that they were having on eternity. Their agreement to remain together contributed to the fulfillment of God's plan for the King of Kings and Lord of Lords to be born into the earth. I encourage you to read the entire story.

Women Serving Women: A Biblical Concept

As you can see from the account above, women leaders who have other women serve them is not a new concept. During biblical times, there were women that served in the households of other women. They were called "handmaids" or "handmaidens." Webster's 1828 Dictionary defines a handmaid as *"a female servant or attendant."*[1] While the title was distinct to women in servitude, it was often used as a way to proclaim or express a posture of humility and submission. Ruth could have been considered the handmaiden of Naomi. She served Naomi by caring for her and submitting to her instruction, which prospered them both. Ruth was not serving Naomi out of obligation, but from a posture of love and humility. This posture is the basis for the title and the heart of this book. There are several examples of handmaids in Scripture:

> "And Laban gave unto his daughter Leah Zilpah his maid for an handmaid. And Laban gave to Rachel his daughter Bilhah his handmaid to be her maid." ***(Zilpah & Bilhah – Genesis 29:24, 29 KJV)***
>
> "And she arose, and bowed herself on her face to the earth, and said, 'Behold, let thine handmaid be a servant to wash the feet of the servants of my lord.'" ***(Abigail, Nabal's wife – 1 Samuel 25:41 KJV)***
>
> "...he hath regarded the low estate of his handmaiden: for, behold, from henceforth all generations shall call me blessed." ***(Mary, the mother of Jesus – Luke 1:48 KJV)***

Scripture reveals that it was part of the culture in Old Testament times for the handmaiden to be given to a woman's husband to bear children for her if she was unable to do so. If you read these accounts in Scripture ***(Genesis 16:1-4, 30:1-3)***, you will note that these decisions were made apart from the counsel of God. This book is in no way suggesting that this act is part of the responsibility of a handmaiden today. It is merely being highlighted so as not to cast a shadow on this work by not addressing it. God is wise and all-knowing, and He included these accounts in His Word for a reason.

> "All Scripture is given by inspiration of God, and is profitable for doctrine, for reproof, for correction, for instruction in righteousness: That the man of God may be perfect, thoroughly furnished unto all good works." ***(2 Timothy 3:16-17 KJV)***

What Is an Armor-Bearer?

During those same biblical time periods, there were men called "armor-bearers." Webster's 1828 Dictionary defines an armor-bearer (also spelled armour-bearer) as *"one who carries the armor of another."*[ii] Dictionary.com defines it as *"a male attendant bearing the armor or arms of a warrior or knight."*[iii] The leader could have been a king, a prince, a captain/commander of an army, or a champion. The armor-bearer went with the leader to carry additional armor in the battle and to guard, defend, and protect the leader during the fight. Also, the armor-bearer killed the wounded enemy soldiers. The Bible gives several examples of armor-bearers:

> *"Then said Saul unto the people that were with him, 'Number now, and see who is gone from us.' And when they had numbered, behold, Jonathan and his armourbearer were not there."* **(1 Samuel 14:17 KJV)**
>
> *"And David came to Saul, and stood before him: and he loved him greatly; and he became his armourbearer."* **(1 Samuel 16:21 KJV)**
>
> *"Zelek the Ammonite, Nahari the Beerothite, armour bearer to Joab the son of Zeruiah."* **(2 Samuel 23:37 KJV)**

When a person in the local church is called an "armor-bearer," it usually means they are someone who has been designated to provide personal support to a senior pastor, his wife (if applicable), or a ministry leader. The title has been adopted and used generically and universally, regardless of gender. There have been several excellent books written on the topic of the armor-bearer and those serving others in this capacity. While the principles offered are very applicable, it seems that they were written *by* men *to* men who *served* men. The Bible makes a clear distinction between the armor-bearer and the handmaiden. My simplified explanation of the distinction is this: An armor-bearer is *"a dude that carries the armor of the king while in battle."* No battle…no armor to carry. A handmaiden is a woman who helps the queen maintain the castle, tend to the "little heirs," and handle other important responsibilities so that the king can focus on the battle.

This book will make a clear distinction between the armor-bearer and the handmaiden by offering a new and fresh perspective on the role of women serving women in leadership. There are so many great women leaders today, and they all have multi-layered responsibilities and complex needs. This book acknowledges the demands placed upon them by providing training to the women that support them.

Women Serving Women: Ladies in Waiting

Women serving women in leadership continued to evolve throughout history. During the Elizabethan era, a woman who served another woman in leadership was called a *lady-in-waiting*. Dictionary.com defines a lady-in-waiting as *"a lady (of the royal household) who attends to a queen or a princess."*[xv] According to the Elizabethan Era Index, ladies-in-waiting were not considered servants and were not required to perform trivial or menial tasks. These were noble companions who, by virtue of their status and nobility, could better advise a woman of high station. The position of a lady-in-waiting was not one that could be applied for. It was a highly prestigious appointment that would only be granted to a woman from a family of nobility and high standing or to someone the queen trusted, such as a relative or an intimate friend. The role of the lady-in-waiting changed and evolved according to the wishes of the reigning monarch and queen. The tradition dates all the way back to the Dark Ages.[v]

While the duties varied from court to court, Elizabethan ladies-in-waiting duties consisted of travelling with Queen Elizabeth I on her frequent processions throughout England, as well as attending state functions and other important occasions. They were expected to be well-versed in etiquette, languages, the latest dances, secretarial tasks, and reading and writing, as they could be required to read and respond to correspondence on behalf of their mistress. They were expected to learn how to embroider, paint, ride, play an instrument, and sing. They would have been in charge of the queen's wardrobe, supervised the servants, kept the mistress abreast of activities and personage at court, and discreetly relayed messages on command.[vi] A lady-in-waiting was not allowed to marry without the consent of the queen.

Ladies-in-waiting are still used today by members of England's royal family. Not all of the women selected are from families of noble birth. Many of them are siblings and close friends. Because of her schedule and strict daily routine, Queen Elizabeth II has nine ladies-in-waiting who serve her. This position is not as stringent as in the past. It is flexible, part-time, and the ladies work in shifts. The position is an unpaid one, although the ladies often receive room and board in the royal residence in London and an allowance for clothing and travel. It is said that these women work without pay because they are usually already wealthy through family or marriage. A lady-in-waiting is expected to serve the queen for life and therefore never retires.

For the sake of organization, there is a hierarchy involved as certain ladies are needed daily, while others are only needed for ceremonial purposes. The senior lady-in-waiting is called the Mistress of the Robe. She is only needed for ceremonial occasions, while others are required more often. The Mistress of the Robe is responsible for the care of the queen's wardrobe and jewelry. She's also in charge of the other ladies-in-waiting and manages their schedule and duties.[vii]

The term "maid of honor" was used to describe a lady-in-waiting who was unmarried. The role of today's maid of honor in a wedding party originated from the lady-in-waiting. While there are some similarities in the duties, much has changed. Historically, the maid of honor attended to the queen or princess during her reign unless she was dismissed. The woman could only become a maid of honor if she was unmarried. Today, the maid of honor attends to the bride until the wedding takes place. Marital status is not a consideration when selecting a maid of honor, although she is usually single; however, a married woman is usually selected as a "matron of honor." The duties are the same. Women are still serving women in leadership today. You are one of them and so am I.

In England, the title *lady-in-waiting* is still used to describe a woman serving another woman in leadership. In America, the position may be called *assistant, personal assistant, executive personal assistant,* or *adjutant*. You may not even have a title. You may be serving your pastor or employer who happens to be a man. There may just be one of you, or a team of women called to serve the first lady of the church. You could be a daughter, mother, sister, or niece, called to serve a relative who is in ministry or business. Your title, relation, or the gender of your leader is not what is important. The value lies in recognizing that God has chosen you *for such a time as this*, to serve those in a leadership position.

POINTS TO PONDER

- The title "armor-bearer" is a generic term that has been adopted by the local church to describe anyone who serves someone in leadership, particularly the senior pastor or first lady. An armor-bearer and a handmaiden are not the same, as they have different roles and responsibilities.

- Women serving women is a concept that has existed for centuries.

- Women leaders come with multilayered responsibilities and complex needs; and for this reason, they need our help.

- Consider the story of Ruth and Naomi. Can you think of areas in your life where you can be more committed?

- Have you placed limits on your commitment to the leader that you serve?

- Do you think that you could be better equipped in your position?

CHAPTER 2

Heaven Has an Agenda

―――♃ ♄―――

"And God said, 'Let us make man in our image, after our likeness: and let them have dominion over the fish of the sea, and over the fowl of the air, and over the cattle, and over all the earth, and over every creeping thing that creepeth upon the earth.' So God created man in his own image, in the image of God created he him; male and female created he them. And God blessed them, and God said unto them, 'Be fruitful, and multiply, and replenish the earth, and subdue it: and have dominion over the fish of the sea, and over the fowl of the air, and over every living thing that moveth upon the earth.'"

(Genesis 1:26-28 KJV)

"Thy kingdom come, thy will be done in earth, as it is in heaven."

(Matthew 6:10 KJV)

THE above Scriptures provide the blueprint for mankind's existence. They establish God as our maker and our life source (father)[i] as well as the purpose for which we were created. When God said, *"Let us make man,"* He was not being gender specific. He was speaking the *entire human race* into existence.

If you notice, God said, *"Let **us**."* When the word "us" is used, you can conclude that there is more than one person involved. The word "us" can also be used in place of the pronouns "we" or "our," all implying more than one. One of the great mysteries of God is that He's three-in-one; thus, the use of the word "us." The making of man was a team effort.

You're Just Like Your Father

God went on to say that the human race was made with two distinct characteristics. We were made *in God's image* and *after His likeness*. Some Bible scholars explain the phrase "being made in His image" as *"exact duplicate of kind."* Image is about identity or *who we were created to be*. Let me use the following illustration to explain. Have you ever made a copy of a document? What happened when you laid the original document down on the copy machine glass, closed the cover, and pressed the start button? The machine produced an exact replica or *duplicate* of your original document. It doesn't matter if you had selected one copy or 1,000 copies—the machine would have reproduced each copy just like the original. And so it is with us. We were all created just like God. And how is God? God is a spirit being and so are we...a teaching for another time.

Scripture also says we were made in the "likeness" of God. Likeness is also about ability or *what we were created to do*. This means that every human being was coded on the inside, with the potential to function or operate just like God. You may be wondering what that means. Have you ever heard someone tell a child, *"You act just like your father?"* What were they saying? They were telling the child that they were exhibiting the same characteristics, nature, or behavior that had been previously demonstrated by their father. The title of father is given to one who *originates, creates, founds,* or *authors* a thing.

Tapping into our full potential *only* becomes possible when we accept God's plan for our lives. We must first embrace our Source and His truths, and then endeavor to learn how God functions or operates. There are specific things that God does; and once we align with Him, we have access (by faith) to the potential within us to do them as well. We are even told in **Ephesians 5:1** to be "imitators of God." (Don't lose interest, I'm going somewhere with this.)

> "When the purpose of something is not known, abuse or abnormal use is inevitable."
> ~Myles Munroe

God's Plan is Heaven's Agenda

In His role as Creator and Redeemer, God established the purpose for everything that He had made, including man. An architect will always create a blueprint before a structure is built. The blueprint serves as a visual aid that establishes all that is required for a structure, to fulfill its purpose for being built; it is a progression used to assist in bringing a concept or idea to life. A blueprint is the *"calling those things that be not as though they were."* There is no guesswork with a blueprint because everything is clearly laid out. The purpose of anything is determined by its creator long before it is ever made; otherwise, its existence would be meaningless. If there is no reason for something to be made, then why make it...who needs it? God declared that everything He made was *good*; but when it came to man, He said the making of him was *very good*! God finished His work of creation and then handed over rulership, ownership, stewardship, and dominion over the earth and everything in it to man.

> *"The heavens belong to the LORD, but he has given the earth to all humanity." **(Psalm 115:16 NLT)***

We have been given delegated authority over the work of God's hands. The only exclusion to this delegation is the right of man to rule over another man. God has given us total control over His earthy creation. He sealed this transfer of authority by limiting Himself of the right to interfere in the affairs of this world or people's personal lives unless expressly invited (by way of prayer) to do so.

God's original intent is heaven's agenda. It was (and still is) God's plan for mankind to reproduce and populate the entire earth with His goodness. Through this population, the entire earth was (and still is) to become a seamless extension and representation of God's Kingdom. This was His plan…to make earth just like heaven. Even Jesus taught his disciples to pray in **Matthew 6:10**, *"Thy Kingdom come, thy will be done, on earth as it is in heaven."*

Long before Jesus arrived on earth, the first man, Adam, messed up big time. He committed an eternity-altering offense that would impact the entire human race. It would also be considered treason against God's Kingdom. He relinquished his authority to an illegal alien spirit disguised as a snake. What Adam did (or rather *didn't* do) caused every man born after him to be doomed to carry his judgment and the sentence of spiritual death through eternal separation from God. Just as one apple seed can produce an apple orchard, so this one seed continues to produce a harvest of walking dead men to this very day.

This surely was not part of heaven's agenda; but God, who is all-seeing and all-knowing, wasn't caught off guard by Eve's deception or Adam's transgression. He was fully aware of the serpent's plot to thwart His eternal plan. He was also just as aware that His very creation would be used against Him as a pawn to try and stop it. He knew that man would fail; that's why He had already committed Himself to restore man back to the high place from which he would ultimately fall.

God, so faithful and steadfast, never lost confidence in His plan *or* His man. (Oh, what great love He has for us!) His agenda…His original intent…His mandate for man to be fruitful, multiply, replenish the earth, and subdue it was (and still is) in effect. God gave us dominion over the earth, and He will never take it back. He expected every man (and woman), starting with Adam, to fulfill his responsibility to dominate the earth.

God's love for the world was manifested in His offering of His Son Jesus as a sacrificial substitute long before the foundation of the world. Jesus would be planted on earth to pay the ultimate price for the transgressions of us all, thereby making it possible for every person to get back into right relationship with Him. He would be the incorruptible seed that would produce a harvest of millions upon millions, just like Himself. The book of **Revelation** confirms that God's plan was in place before time began:

> *"And I beheld, and, lo, in the midst of the throne and of the four beasts, and in the midst of the elders, stood a Lamb as it had been slain, having seven horns and seven eyes, which are the seven Spirits of God sent forth into all the earth."*
> **(Revelation 5:6 KJV)**

"And all that dwell upon the earth shall worship him, whose names are not written in the book of life of the Lamb slain from the foundation of the world." (**Revelation 13:8 KJV**)

Did you know that our God is a wise investment banker? He is never wasteful. The planting of Jesus Christ wasn't some altruistic thing that God decided to do. He is always looking for *profit*...not *prophet*. Why do you think He told Adam and Eve in our opening chapter verse that they were to *"be fruitful and multiply?"* God is expecting a huge return on His investment. He made an investment in Adam, Eve, and *us* by giving us dominion over the earth. God is expecting us to produce (*be fruitful*) and multiply (*increase exponentially, expanding at a rapid pace*). Scripture confirms this:

"Thus saith the LORD, thy Redeemer, the Holy One of Israel; 'I am the LORD thy God which teacheth thee to profit, which leadeth thee by the way that thou shouldest go.'" (**Isaiah 48:17 KJV**)

"And he called his ten servants, and delivered them ten pounds, and said unto them, 'Occupy till I come.'" (**Luke 19:13 KJV**) (Note: Occupy means *"to advance and hold"* in this context.)

God's plan for man will never change. It is just as real today as it was when He spoke it. What He decreed, He won't renege on...He *can't*, because He esteems what He has said higher than His own name.

"I will worship toward thy holy temple, and praise thy name for thy lovingkindness and for thy truth: for thou hast magnified thy word above all thy name." (**Psalm 138:2 KJV**)

The problem is that God can't do it Himself because He is bound by His commitment to allow man to rule the earth. Therefore, He must find those who will partner with Him to bring heaven to earth; those whom He can empower to express His love and goodness to a dying world; those He can trust to execute justice on earth; those He can send into the marketplace and to represent Him in every pillar or mountain that makes up our society and change the existing cultures to that of His Kingdom.

God's Kingdom Is at Hand

As a believer in Jesus Christ, you've got to understand things from His point of view. Failure to do so will result in your inability to fully participate and reap the full benefit of what He did, to make eternal life available to you. It also has everything to do with how you see yourself and perceive serving your leader. Let me explain. Jesus' point of view is a KINGDOM point of view. We all know that He is the King of Kings and Lord of Lords…and you cannot be a king without a kingdom. Jesus never preached about religion or Christianity. The subject of Jesus' first sermon at the start of His ministry can be found in **Matthew 4:17**: *"From that time Jesus began to preach, and to say, 'Repent: for the kingdom of heaven is at hand.'"*

He came telling people to *"repent"* or *"change the way they think."* Why is that important? Because Jesus' point of view includes how He sees you. Your willingness to embrace His point of view will determine what you are able to receive from God. You may be wondering how Jesus sees you. He sees you as a citizen of His Kingdom **(Philippians 3:20 AMP)**. Your constitution is the Bible, which details your rights, benefits, and responsibilities. You are part of a commonwealth, which means that your

King is responsible for your well-being. You have been appointed as an ambassador for Christ *(2 Corinthians 5:20)*, with diplomatic responsibilities and immunity. You are part of a government that is backed by an angelic military, responsible for your protection and well-being. You are expected to represent Jesus as your King and His Kingdom well in whatever you do. (I would like to encourage you to take the time and do an in-depth study on this subject. It will change your life.)

You have been strategically assigned by God as a handmaiden in the service of your leader. This is your place of dominion. It's your sphere of influence. It's the place where you exercise your ambassadorship! It's where you are expected to be fruitful, multiply, replenish the earth, and subdue it. It's where your gifts will manifest. It's where your anointing will flow. It's the place of "no toil" because you are where you're supposed to be…on purpose! Heaven has an agenda, and you are an integral part in the fulfillment of it!

> *"What are mere mortals that you should think about them, human beings that you should care for them? Yet you made them only a little lower than God and crowned them with glory and honor. You gave them charge of everything you made, putting all things under their authority."* **(Psalm 8:4-6 NLT)**

> *"Asked by the Pharisees when the Kingdom of God would come, He replied to them saying, 'The Kingdom of God does not come with signs to be observed or with visible display. Nor will people say "Look! Here [it is]!" or, "See [it is] there!" For behold, the kingdom of God is within you [in your hearts] and among you [surrounding you].'"* **(Luke 17:20-21 AMP)**

"Listen to the truth I speak: 'Whoever does not open their arms to receive God's Kingdom like a teachable child will never enter it.'" ***(Mark 10:15 TPT)***

POINTS TO PONDER

- You were made in the image and likeness of God, which means you have the *potential* to function like Him.

- To find your true purpose requires that you ask the One who made you—God.

- God's plan is to make earth an extension of His Kingdom. Read **Isaiah 9:6-7**.

- You are a citizen of God's Kingdom **(Philippians 3:20)**, which gives you rights, benefits, and responsibilities. Do you know what they are?

- Your assignment as a handmaiden to your leader is directly connected to heaven's agenda.

- You are also an ambassador of God's Kingdom **(2 Corinthians 5:20)**. As His ambassador, God expects you to represent Him everywhere you go and in everything you do.

CHAPTER 3

God Needs Women Too!

> "...When God created man, He made him in the likeness of God. He created them male and female and blessed them and named them [both] Adam [Man] at the time they were created."
>
> ***(Genesis 5:1b-2 AMPC)***
>
> "And Adam called his wife's name Eve; because she was the mother of all living."
>
> ***(Genesis 3:20 KJV)***

Women's Rights: The Bible

God always intended for women to be an integral part of His plan. Before there was a physical Adam and Eve, *"He called their name Adam,"* and He blessed them. He empowered them both to make a difference in their world. But we all know about the huge mistake that Eve made. She foolishly had a conversation with a snake (Satan incarnate), who conned her into believing that God was deliberately withholding something from her and Adam. For reasons unknown, Adam didn't exercise his authority. Instead, he allowed himself to be talked into violating a direct command from God. His silence led him to sin, which ultimately infected the entire human race.

God understood the ramifications of what Adam and Eve had done, yet He didn't sideline Eve. Though there were consequences, she was still *the mother of all living things*. God never intended for all of the women who would come after her to be sidelined either. When God said, *"be fruitful and multiply,"* His mandate wasn't just confined to procreation for population. In other words, God's declaration to "be fruitful" went far beyond having babies. He equipped women with everything they need to do so much more. The problem has been that the enemy of all mankind has done everything he can to suppress women and continues to do so. He is very aware that God gave mankind dominion over all the earth, and that the need to rule is inherent in us all. The enemy knows that if he can manipulate us, we will dominate each other, even though God never sanctioned this type of rule. That's why when a person, people group, or society has tried to suppress or oppress another person or people group (like women), those being suppressed rebelled. We've had plenty of opportunity in 2020 to see this stark reality played out in our cities and our world as people protest the injustices of our day. Sadly, the suppression and oppression of women is nothing new. It has been woven into the fabric of many cultures throughout history and still exists today.

During biblical times, women were not esteemed by men, but God still used them mightily. Before the birth of Christ, God used women like Sarah ***(Genesis 21)***, Rahab ***(Joshua 2:1-24)***, Deborah ***(Judges 4, 5)***, Hannah ***(1 Samuel 1, 2)***, and Esther

(Book of Esther) to change the course of history. God used a young girl named Mary to supernaturally conceive and carry the Christ Child *(Luke 1-2)*, and He used the prophetess Anna who stayed in the temple day and night to pray forth His arrival into the earth *(Luke 2:36-37)*.

There was the Samaritan woman who became the first evangelist *(John 4)*. It was a group of women that followed Jesus to Galilee so that they could serve Him. Many (if not all) of these same women used their substance to finance Jesus' ministry *(Matthew 27:55-56; Luke 8:1-3)*. How could they do it if they weren't women of means? Some of these same women went by faith to Jesus' tomb to care for His body after His crucifixion. (He wasn't there, Hallelujah!) Mary Magdalene was one of these women who had seven demons cast out of her by Jesus. He later trusted her to go and tell His disciples that He had risen! *(Mark 16)*

In the days of the New Testament apostles, there were many anointed women who were actively involved in the expansion of the early church. Priscilla, who was a tentmaker, with her husband, Aquilla *(Acts 18:1-3)*. Lydia was a seller of purple (a wealthy woman) who opened her home to the apostle Paul *(Acts 16:14)*. Phoebe (her name means "bright and radiant") was highly regarded by the apostle Paul. He referred to her as a deaconess (servant) and a succorer (helper) in the church. It is said that she was also his emissary, delivering his letter to the believers in Rome *(Romans 16: 1-2, 27)*.

There are many more women in the Bible that I wasn't able to highlight. If you've never done so, I would encourage you to study the New Testament women, especially those you have never heard of before. You'll be surprised how influential they were in the growth of the early Church.

Women's Rights: The Roman Empire

Ancient Rome's participation in multiple wars resulted in a great loss of men and a financial burden being placed upon its government. Many of the wives and daughters of the dead men became very wealthy from the inheritances they received. The government decided that it would make up its financial deficits from the resources of these women by passing the Oppian Law, which limited the amount of gold that these women could own to half an ounce. They were not allowed to wear dresses trimmed in purple (really!) because purple denoted wealth, and when the women wore it, it reminded the government of how much it had lost. They were also not allowed to ride in horse-drawn carriages in Rome or in towns nearby. After some towns outside of the city had lifted these restrictions, a tribunal was eventually formed to consider repealing the law. Some members of the tribunal had decided to veto the repeal until the women of Rome united in public protest. The pending veto was withdrawn, and the repeal of the Oppian Law was approved.[i]

Women's Rights: America

In America during the 1800s, the mindset of "a woman's place being in the home" was the basis for denying women the right to vote or to hold any kind of public office. If women didn't conform to this mindset, they were not considered "pious" or devoutly religious. It didn't matter that women were taking the lead in fighting for the abolishment of slavery and establishing moral reform in our nation. They were placed in the same category as those they were fighting for. This inequality eventually became the fuel that ignited the flame for the women's suffrage (right to vote) movement. It would take decades before the 19th Amendment was finally passed, giving women the legal right to vote.[ii] Though they actively contributed to the success of the women's suffrage movement, Black women were excluded from the 19th amendment, not in principle, but in practice. They were eventually granted the right to vote, after being thwarted in their efforts to do so for many years.

In the 1960s, another movement arose called the "Women's Rights Movement," (also known as the "Women's Liberation Movement") based largely in the United States. Women sought equal rights and opportunities, and greater personal freedom. It coincided with and is recognized as part of the "second wave" of feminism. (The women's suffrage movement was considered the first wave.) The Women's Rights Movement touched every area of a woman's experience including politics, work, family, and sexuality. This type of organized activism by and on behalf of women continued through the third and fourth waves of feminism from the mid-1990s to the early 2000s. I am not going to take the time to discuss them here—I am sharing this information as historical facts. *These are not my personal beliefs or political position.* My point is that I am endeavoring to heighten a deeper truth of what happens when people try to dominate other people.[iii]

Since 2017, thousands of women have come out of hiding under the social media hashtag #MeToo and banded together to share their stories of widespread sexual abuse in the marketplace, specifically in the entertainment industry. The "Me Too" movement was started by Tarana Burke, who, as a counselor at a youth camp, came face-to-face with sexual abuse involving a young girl. Tarana, haunted by her own memories of childhood abuse, directed the girl to go talk to someone else she believed was better equipped to help her. She experienced tremendous guilt for rejecting the young girl and not having the courage to tell her *"me too."* After dealing with her own issues, she began using the phrase "me too" to raise awareness of the pervasiveness of sexual abuse and assault in our society.[iv] According to metoomvmt.org, the movement was founded by Tarana in 2006 to "help survivors of sexual violence, particularly black women and girls, and other young women of color from low wealth communities, find pathways to healing."[v] This movement is still going on as of this writing. [iv] According to ***John 3:16***...*all* lives which He created matter to God!

Women's Rights: The Local Church

The local church has not been exempt from the unfair treatment of women. While tremendous progress has been made, in many churches (especially more traditional ones), women are still being prohibited from serving in certain capacities. There is still the unspoken belief that "a woman's place is in the home."

This mindset is based primarily on these Scriptures:

> *God didn't just call women to the bedroom...He also called us to His throne room and to the boardroom!*

> *"Let your women keep silence in the churches: for it is not permitted unto them to speak; but they are commanded to be under obedience as also saith the law." (**1 Corinthians 14:34 KJV**)*

> *"I do not permit a woman to teach or to assume authority over a man; she must be quiet." (**1 Timothy 2:12 NIV**)*

These Scriptures have been debated for years. The question of whether women should hold leadership positions in the church has always been controversial. Apostle Paul did say these things; but what was the context in which he said them and is it relevant now? I'm not here to debate these Scriptures—there are many points of view on what Paul meant and whether it applies today. What I do know is that *any Scripture applied with the wrong motive can become a stumbling block instead of a liberator.* Sadly, instead of God's Words being used as keys of His Kingdom to set people free, they are used as keys to deny women access to the opportunity to become the full expression of who God created them to be. Jesus did not look well upon people who became roadblocks to others *(Matthew 23, Luke 11).* Unfortunately, women who love God have been...and *are still...*being denied the right to be all that God has called them to be. I know...because *it happened to me.* I was one of those women for a very long time.

I believe that Satan has taken the opportunity to use this mindset to strategically work against a very important group of women...pastors and ministers' wives, especially those in more traditional churches. I remember my early days in the church. We would frequently go to different churches for "evening programs" so I got a chance to see many pastors' wives. The pastor's wives, or "first ladies" as they are called, were known for their attire. No matter the occasion, they would be beautifully dressed in sparkly suits, matching shoes, and a big fancy matching hat. They would sit on the front row like beautiful birds, perched in gilded cages. Seen...but not *heard. Tolerated...*but not *celebrated.* Having the *right outward demeanor...*but *suffering in silence.* Doing what was *expected...*but not *respected.* Never allowed to be who God intended. Living in the shadow of their husband's work.

The only time we got to hear anything from the pastors' wives was during the annual "Women's Day" program which usually lasted the weekend. During this time, they would step out and shine! Once the weekend was over, they would retreat back into their gilded cages to once again be seen and not heard. It was the same protocol in every church, and all of the first ladies that I met were treated the same way. They all followed the same pattern as the other pastor's wives in their circle. It was like they had no identity of their own. Sadly, it reminded me of the movie *The Stepford Wives*. This had a disturbing effect upon me because as a young woman in the church, these women were my examples and being like them was what I was supposed to aspire to.

Being a first lady was never viewed as a calling…it was more of a status symbol. There were many of these women who were comfortable with it and wore it well; but there were others who didn't, especially those who were young first ladies. This is not a criticism, but my own observation as a young woman coming up in the church. For those of you who have come up in this type of environment, you can attest to what I've shared.

I want to make it clear that I'm not categorizing all churches or first ladies as being the same. My church and first lady are not like what I described, and I know of others who are different as well. There are many first ladies who are satisfied with where they are and what they are doing…and God bless them. What I *am* saying is that there are women who are a part of the church of Jesus Christ who are still being suppressed.

Women's Rights: My Story

When I first gave my heart to the Lord and started going to church consistently, I noticed that the women in the church, especially those called to leadership/ministry (which included the pastor's wives), were treated differently than men. The most women were able to do was to make announcements, sing in the choir, be on the nurses or mothers board, teach Sunday school, or prepare and serve meals in the kitchen. If you had a needed skill, you would certainly be asked to use it, but the spirit of religion and tradition would not let the women be acknowledged as a ministry gift to the Body of Christ. To demonstrate the inequity, women were not allowed to sit or stand behind the podium in the pulpit. There was also an unspoken rule that women could only use the podium that sat on the floor to the side of the main podium to make announcements. Even if it was their annual Women's Day celebration, the guest speaker had to give her message from the lower podium.

If a woman demonstrated any type of spiritual leadership, she would be slapped with the title of "evangelist," even if she had never been any place or led anyone to Christ. I remember going to a church to visit, and I was introduced as "Evangelist Carlie." I would get so annoyed when people would address me as "Evangelist," because I knew that the spirits of religion and tradition were behind it. I'm not confused. I know that an *"evangelist"* is one of the five-fold ministry gifts set in the church by God for the perfecting of the saints according to **Ephesians 4:18**. I also know that we are all evangelists from the standpoint that we should all be leading people to Jesus. But I resented people trying to put me in their religious boxes. I felt that I was being suppressed, and I rebelled against it.

When my family and I moved to another part of Chicago, we joined my husband's home church, where his family still attended. We served there faithfully until God impressed on us to leave and go help a new pastor at another church. After being there for some years, God really started tugging at my heart about my calling into ministry, but I didn't know what to do about it. After talking with my husband, I was led to speak to my pastor. Mind you; by this time, I wasn't a baby believer. I had become one of the church's Sunday school teachers. I've always loved God's Word, so it was natural for me to teach Sunday school. I didn't know at the time that being a "teacher" was a five-fold ministry gift. I only had three or four students, if that many, but I loved it so much that I would prepare as if there were thousands of students in my class. I was so hungry for God's Word that I would spend most of my free time listening to my current pastor (who was not my pastor at the time) and others, including Dr. Charles Stanley and Frederick KC Price. God used them to build the solid biblical foundation on which I stand today. I was also ministering to women with substance abuse issues.

My husband tried to discourage me from talking to the pastor. I didn't quite understand why; but in an effort to keep the peace, I told my husband that I wouldn't go to him…but that if *he* approached *me*, I would bring up the subject. Well, one morning, I was in the church kitchen getting breakfast when the pastor approached and asked me if I would come to his office. (Don't tell *me* that God won't orchestrate some stuff!) I went to the pastor's office and sat down. I don't even remember why he called me to his office or what he wanted to talk to me about—I just remember telling him that I believed that God was calling me into ministry, and I didn't know what to do about it. As my pastor, I was looking to him for guidance.

He got so quiet that you could hear a pin drop. I was sitting across from him, waiting on a response; and he finally looked at me and told me in his "religious voice" that the Holy Spirit had not said anything to him about me going into ministry. That was his answer. Nothing else. He didn't offer to pray for me or with me for God's direction and timing. He didn't even tell *me* to pray about it. Not one word of encouragement…nothing. He basically said that because *he* hadn't heard it that what I sensed was irrelevant. In other words…*I missed God!* It's like I said, when people are being suppressed or oppressed, rebellion at some point will be next. I thanked him and politely told him that I wasn't looking for his validation, but that I was seeking direction. Then I walked out of his office. I was crushed! I expected more from my pastor…and it didn't stop there.

The following week, my husband and I went to Bible study. The pastor came in and said he was starting a new teaching series called, *"Why God Has Not Called Women to Preach,"* and guess what Scriptures he used? I was *floored!* I couldn't believe what he was doing, but I *refused* to give in to this blatant attack on my calling. Looking straight ahead, stone faced and fighting back tears, I was declaring on the inside that I would not let him see me cry. There was *no way* that I was going to sit through this so-called "Bible study" and be humiliated. I refused to believe that God would do something like this. When it was over, my husband and I got up and left. Even my husband knew that what had just taken place was not right; and when we got in the car, I told him that I was not going back to Bible study. He was silent.

My heart was hurting, but I went back to church. I left the choir, gave up my Sunday school class, and quit counting money. I was cordial to the pastor, but I avoided him as much as possible. I wanted to run away from the church, but my husband wasn't ready to leave. He was in a position of authority, and he had a close relationship with the pastor. I knew I couldn't just leave—I had to wait until God spoke to my husband. If I left and we weren't in agreement, I would be outside of the will of God. I had heard of married couples agreeing to go to separate churches, but that wasn't going to be our story.

I would be fine until Saturday night—then my whole demeanor would change because I dreaded going to church. I would go, sit in the pew, and watch. I watched as a boy of seventeen was welcomed to sit in the pulpit with the pastor because his mother said that God had called him into the ministry. I watched as the associate pastor regularly stumbled into church reeking of alcohol and cigarette smoke as he passed, to go and sit in the pulpit with the other pastors and ministers. I was *so* angry about what was going on, but I decided to humble myself and keep going back. I kept praying for release.

It took six months; but one day, my husband came to me and said he understood how I felt and was going to meet with the pastor. After the meeting, he told me that I could start looking for a new church home for our family. We continued to attend there until the Lord directed us to a new church. Our family visited it one time and agreed that it was our new home…and that is where we are today. Thank you, Jesus! There is nothing the enemy of mankind can do that will hinder God's plan for man…or woman!

Let me stop right here and emphasize that *I am not bashing men.* I love one. I honor and respect the men that God has placed in authority. Why? Because God has a divine order established in His Kingdom according to **1 Corinthians 11:3** which says, *"But I would have you to know, that the head of every man is Christ, and the head of the woman is the man and the head of Christ is God."* This Scripture is very clear. God has placed man in the positions of headship and leadership. He is the head, and he is responsible and will be held accountable to lead. Our God is a God of order, and *we must respect this order, for in it there is divine protection.* Refusing to submit to God's divine order is a disruption of heaven's way of doing things. Dishonor is a violation of kingdom protocol. Who said we can't be great and still submit to our husbands or to those whom God has placed in authority over us? We must honor the men in our lives. We can never be *in* authority if we are unwilling to be *under* authority. We must learn to follow before we can lead!

I want to bring home the point that when God said, *"Let us make man,"* women were not excluded. God created both men and women to be just like Him, equally, with the potential to display His character and nature. One was not created superior to the other. A man and a woman are distinct only in their physical structure, levels of authority, roles, and areas of responsibility.

In a biblically modeled marriage, a wife is instructed to submit to her husband because someone has to "yield" so that there can be order. I could easily have rebelled against my husband and not gone back to our church, and the eyes of some people I would have been justified because I had been ostracized and humiliated during Bible study. But I decided to humble (*yield*) myself and continue to go with the right attitude, because I understood that my yielding was a *spiritual* matter, not a *natural* one. This also holds true in your relationship with your leader. Yielding is important…*especially* during times when you may not understand or agree with decisions that are being made.

Have you ever driven up to a stop sign at the same time as someone else? What would happen if you ignored one another and kept driving? There would be a fender bender for sure. Someone has to Y-I-E-L-D! The other person's car is no better than yours. They both have four wheels, doors, windows, seats, etc. Each car may be equally important to their respective owner; but if someone doesn't yield, everyone involved will be calling their insurance company. God would not have required the wife to submit (yield) to her husband if she was inferior. Anything with two heads is a freak; and without order, there will always be CHAOS!

I have visited numerous churches and have seen many more church congregations via social media, and it is undeniable that the largest people group in most churches today is women…and they are supporting the work of the church through their giving. They should be allowed to use their gifts, callings, talents, and skills to expand God's Kingdom if they desire to do so. I believe that God intended for us to *serve* and *submit* to His divine order, but *not* to be *suppressed* because of it. Sadly, too many women are.

This is *not* about feminism or gender bias. These are human ideologies that are overshadowed by the plans of God. It is the will of God that every believer, male *and* female, take their rightful place and get about doing their part to advance His Kingdom. The Scriptures give us an excellent analogy in **1 Corinthians 12**. Part of the chapter reads:

> *"But that isn't the way God has made us. He has made many parts for our bodies and has put each part just where he wants it. What a strange thing a body would be if it had only one part! So he has made many parts, but still there is only one body. The eye can never say to the hand, 'I don't need you.' The head can't say to the feet, 'I don't need you.' Now here is what I am trying to say: All of you together are the one body of Christ, and each one of you is a separate and necessary part of it."* **(1 Corinthian 12:18-21, 27 NLT)**

The Women's Hall of Faith

As we have gone down through the halls of history, we have seen the value that God places on women and how Satan has attempted to suppress them. If God didn't need women, why has there always been such an effort to stop them? There is no way Satan can stop us because we are part of a more powerful body. Jesus declared that *the gates of hell shall not prevail against His church*, which is *His people*...which *includes women*! God has a federation of godly women that continues to grow daily. There are forerunners such as abolitionist Harriet Tubman, Christian activist Corrie ten Boom, Evangelist Maria Woodworth-Etter, Evangelist Kathryn Kuhlman, and Missionary Mother Teresa. And present-day giants like Dr. Veronica Winston, Prophet Cindy Jacobs, Marilyn Hickey, Pastor Sheryl Brady, Joyce Meyer, Dr. Cindy Trimm, Dr. Patricia Bailey, Christine Caine, Gloria Copeland, Dr. Heidi Baker, Dr. Paula Price, and Jane Harmon who will be passing the torch to the next generation. This list is ever increasing.

These are very well-known women of faith, yet there is still an army of women on earth that are working faithfully to advance God's Kingdom. They may not be as *notable*, but they are no less *noble*. They may be relatively unknown to some but are very well known by heaven. They are enlightened to the truth of God's Word and therefore free from the confines of misused Scriptures, actively pursuing a higher purpose...God's business. They are influencing their assigned regions and affecting change in their spheres of influence. They are married, divorced, widowed, single, millennial, seasoned, black, white, brown, red, etc. Some of these women have laid down their own lives, dreams, and aspirations to work alongside their husbands, supporting them in fulfilling the assignment that God has given them, while others run their own churches/ministries or have leadership responsibilities in business, government, media, arts and entertainment, family, and education.

Women are making an impact on every mountain that makes up our society. If you talk to these women, you will find that they have multiple responsibilities. In addition to their profession, they are wives, mothers, grandmothers, and guardians, responsible for the well-being of others. Every one of these women, whether notable or unknown, working in ministry or the marketplace; or taking care of the home—is special to God. They have been called to lead in their respective spheres of influence, and they deserve to be treated with the dignity, honor, and respect that their position of leadership deserves.

God Has Called You

And what about you? Are you wondering where you fit in God's great plan? What is your role, assignment, or responsibility? Well, guess what? *God needs you*, Woman! HE HAS CALLED YOU TO SERVE WOMEN LEADERS. Whether you work alone or with a team, just like Queen Esther, *you have been summoned by God for such a time as this*.

God has chosen you to share His goodness by serving the leader He's assigned you to. Again, this isn't just for women serving other women in ministry. You may be serving a woman leader in the marketplace. Even if the woman you serve is not born again, God has chosen you to be the light that may guide her to Him through the way in which you serve her. God has called you as a *change agent…a problem-solver…a solutionist*. You are the go-to person that your leader needs by her side to get the job done! When Daniel and the Hebrew boys were taken into captivity, God gave them such knowledge and skill in all understanding and wisdom that they were found to be ten times better than their counterparts. I prophesy that the same anointing that rested upon Daniel and the Hebrew boys will come upon you if you dare to ask God for it. You will provide solutions to problems that will cause your leader to inquire how you have such knowledge...it will be the open door for you to share your faith. *GOD HAS CALLED **YOU**!*

As the handmaiden of a woman in leadership, you have been called to serve a specific purpose, and what you do is contributing to heaven, fulfilling its agenda. I know this may be news to some of you. This may be the first time that you've looked at what you do from this perspective. You may have *no idea* how much value you bring to the table. If you do, praise God! Let this reinforce what you may already know in your heart. If you don't, you need to know that *GOD NEEDS **YOU**!*

> **Serving your leader contributes to the fulfillment of heaven's agenda.**

If you have the desire to serve and feel that your purpose in life is to undergird, support, and encourage another leader, then *GOD HAS CALLED **YOU**!*

These great women have so much to do and so little time. How do they get it all done? *GOD HAS CALLED **YOU**!*

Because of the position that these powerful women hold, there aren't many they can allow into their "inner circle." Who can they trust to let into their personal life? *GOD HAS CALLED **YOU**!*

Some of these fantastic women are in roles that require that they travel. They shouldn't have to be out there alone. Who can

God trust to go with them? *GOD HAS CALLED* **YOU***!*

Sometimes, it can be those "little things" that hinder these incredible women from focusing on the bigger things. Who can take those little things off their hands? *GOD HAS CALLED* **YOU***!*

People are always in need of something from these wonderful women: prayer, direction, decision, financial support, feedback, instruction, etc. Who will help to meet their needs? *GOD HAS CALLED* **YOU***!*

These compassionate women spend so much time encouraging others. Who will encourage them? Who will pray for them? *GOD HAS CALLED* **YOU***!*

These marvelous women need honesty just like anyone else, but they know that because of who they are, people don't always tell them the truth. Who will be honest with them? *GOD HAS CALLED* **YOU***!*

These mighty women of God make great sacrifices. They give out so much. Who will be there when they need support? *GOD HAS CALLED* **YOU***!*

These extraordinary leaders who are working in ministry and the marketplace, giving so much of their time, talents, and treasures, yet asking for so little for themselves in return... *GOD HAS CALLED* **YOU** *TO SERVE THEM!*

> **All that you do today is making room for your tomorrow.**

Let me make this point: just because your position is to serve, don't think for a minute that you're not considered an *amazing, great, powerful, fantastic, incredible, wonderful, compassionate, marvelous, mighty, extraordinary* woman yourself. You are special to God too! There's none like you. When God made you, He broke the mold! It takes a special someone to provide the service you do. Sure, you have dreams, plans, and aspirations. And yes, there are things you want to do and places you want to go. Yet you have chosen to lay aside a portion of your life for the sake of serving your leader. God sees *everything*…and He keeps good records!

I'm speaking prophetically because of your service to your leader. God will empower you, enlarge you, and make it possible for you to fulfill His plan for your life. The sacrifice you are making will surely affect the lives of many. What you do today has eternal implications. It's making room for your tomorrow. God's plan for your life is not separate from your service to your leader…it is in concert with it! All that you do today is in preparation for what lies ahead.

I found a powerful statement by Matthew Henry in his Bible Commentary on **1 Kings 19:19-21** that says, *"Those that would be fit to teach must have time to learn, and those that hope hereafter to rise and rule must be willing to first stoop and serve."*

No matter our station in life, as women, we all have a part to play in fulfilling God's mandate. God needs women, and we are expected to do our part. It's our responsibility to seek the face of God to find out what that part is. As you willingly choose to lay down your life for the benefit of serving your leader, you can be assured that God will empower and enlarge you for all that you do. See what you do as your opportunity to place a demand on the potential that's inside of you. See this as a chance to utilize your gifts for the glory of God. See this as an opportunity to be a blessing to God's woman leader and those she will impact because of you!

"A capable, intelligent, and virtuous woman—who is he who can find her? She is far more precious than jewels and her value is far above rubies or pearls." **(Proverbs 31:10 AMPC)**

"There is neither **Jew** nor **Greek**, there is neither **bond** nor **free**, there is neither **male** nor **female**: for ye are all one in Christ Jesus." **(Galatians 3:28 KJV)**

"Greater love hath no man than this, that a man lay down his life for his friends." **(John 15:13 KJV)**

POINTS TO PONDER

- God doesn't bench you when you make a mistake. He will use you even in your imperfections.

- When God said, *"Be fruitful and multiply,"* he wasn't just talking about making babies. He was talking about being productive as well. Are you as productive as you can be?

- The funding of Jesus' ministry by women of means should remove the "myth" that God is against His people being rich.

- Women have always been actively involved in addressing societal issues.

- The Word of God is meant to set people free; but if misused, it can just as easily put people in bondage.

- Search the New Testament Scriptures, and see how many other women leaders or influencers you can find. I'll give you one: Dorcas.

CHAPTER 4

Handpicked by God

"And there came an angel of the LORD, and sat under an oak which was in Ophrah, that pertained unto Joash the Abiezrite: and his son Gideon threshed wheat by the winepress, to hide it from the Midianites. And the angel of the LORD appeared unto him, and said unto him, 'The LORD is with thee, thou mighty man of valor.' And Gideon said unto him, 'Oh my Lord, if the LORD be with us, why then is all this befallen us? and where be all his miracles which our fathers told us of, saying, "Did not the LORD bring us up from Egypt?" but now the LORD hath forsaken us, and delivered us into the hands of the Midianites.' And the LORD looked upon him, and said, 'Go in this thy might, and thou shalt save Israel from the hand of the Midianites: have not I sent thee?' And he said unto him, 'Oh my Lord, wherewith shall I save Israel? Behold, my family is poor in Manasseh, and I am the least in my father's house.' And the LORD said unto him, 'Surely I will be with thee, and thou shalt smite the Midianites as one man.'"

(Judges 6:11-16 KJV)

GOD chose Gideon to free the children of Israel from the oppressive Amalekites. Gideon had been handpicked by God to fulfill a very important task, and an angel appeared to him to deliver the news concerning his new assignment. The angel's initial greeting to Gideon spoke to the fear, resentment toward God, and low self-esteem that plagued his soul. Gideon's response validated the need for the angel's decree. What came out of his heart was an indictment against God. He blamed the absence of God's presence for his present condition, all the while seeking justice in his accusation of the missing miracles that his ancestors had rehearsed in his hearing so many times before. The verses started out talking about the angel of the Lord and then switched to the Lord speaking directly to Gideon (Verse 14). *Gideon was so focused on his circumstances that he couldn't see the miracle that was standing right before his very eyes!*

Gideon had a supernatural encounter with Almighty God Himself, but he was so busy complaining that he couldn't see that God was making *him* the solution to his problem!

> **What we consider to be a mess can actually be our miracle!**

God told Gideon to go and deliver His people. Gideon tried hard to disqualify himself by detailing all of his flaws to his creator, *the one who made him perfectly.* When Gideon tried to make excuses, God simply ignored him (and his excuses!) He had already declared to Gideon that he was a *"mighty man of valor," (Judges 6:12 KJV)* and *He wasn't taking it back!* Instead, God assured Gideon that He, the Lord, would be with him. And He was! How is it that God picked Gideon to be a deliverer with all his fear issues?

> *"For we are God's [own] handiwork (His workmanship), recreated in Christ Jesus, [born anew] that we may do those good works which God predestined (planned beforehand) for us [taking paths which He prepared ahead of time], that we should walk in them [living the good life which He prearranged and made ready for us to live]."* **(Ephesians 2:10 AMPC)**

When God looks at you, He doesn't see the person that you see. He *sees* you how He *made* you. He sees the person that He created you to be. He sees you through the eyes of heaven's persona. That's why personal prophecy is so valuable. When someone speaks a prophetic word to us, *they are speaking into our lives what God knows about us*. What He has to do is get us to agree with who He says we *are*, what He says we can *do*, and what He says we can *have*. We can only do this by faith.

I will never forget how God led me to the position that I am in today. I started by just giving my time. Our church has a Helps Ministry Fair every summer. It is a time when all the Helps Ministries set up displays designed to recruit new people to serve. Each ministry has a booth that is decorated to represent the group's uniqueness. It's really a sight to see all of the creativity that is put into the various presentations. In one of our more recent years, the engineers rigged a sink that was suspended in mid-air with running water. I'm still trying to figure that one out!

In 2000, the fair was not as large and elaborate as it is today. It was held on a Sunday evening in the church sanctuary and the Women's Fellowship Ministry had a table on display. There were so many women surrounding the table that I couldn't see anything, so I just stuck my arm in between two sisters, grabbed copies of all of the papers that were there, and stuffed them in my bag. When I got home from work the next day, I pulled the papers out to take a look at them, and one page was a job description for the position of Director of Women's Fellowship. The list of responsibilities filled the page. On November 30, 2000 (the day after the fair), I wrote the following note in my journal: *"This job is really a stretch, but I believe it's **my** job because I have been asking God to open a door so I could work at the church to help the first lady."* I also wrote, *"I had just told my husband last night (the night before the fair) that I wanted to work for the church to help her."*

What I didn't realize was that my journal entry was prophesying my future. The job description I grabbed off the table was not a paid position…yet my entry called it a job *twice*. I had no idea that one day I would actually be employed at the church; but it was a desire of my heart and God eventually granted it. I've come to understand that God wasn't interested in giving me a job…He had something greater in mind. He was interested in giving me an opportunity to be a part of something much bigger than myself, but I needed to prove my faithfulness by serving without expecting anything in return. (Another teaching for another time!)

The first lady and I spoke five days later, and she asked me three questions so that she could hear what was on my heart. I was supposed to have nine days to come up with the answers because I had to go out of town on a business trip, but with our conflicting schedules, we weren't able to speak again until January 19, 2001.

Finally, on February 16, I journaled this entry: *"I checked the answering machine and received a message from First Lady. She called yesterday and wants to meet with me on Saturday at 10:00 a.m. so we can make the transition. I'm the new Director of Women's Fellowship!"* I didn't call her until the next day because I hadn't checked our answering machine! I wonder if anyone still has one? LOL!

Our meeting was scheduled for the day after I listened to the message. We prayed, then we talked and planned; we prayed some more, and the rest is history. Even though the job description still seemed daunting on paper, especially after our meeting, I knew in my heart that I was in the right place. In 2001, I started out by giving my time to help my first lady. Today (twenty years at publication), I am on staff as her personal assistant. How did it happen? I was handpicked by heaven!

> *"You did not choose Me, but I chose you. I selected you so that you would go and produce fruit, and your fruit would remain. Then the Father will give you whatever you ask in My name."* **(John 15:16 TLV)**

Depending upon the size and complexity of your church, ministry, or organization, you may not have been given a training manual for how to do what you are expected to do. You may not even have a job description for your position or anyone to go to as a resource. It could be a case where the position is brand new. Also, serving individuals is quite different from serving an organization. Each person has their own personality, specific needs, desires, and expectations. Don't despair, because you have the Holy Spirit (and this book!) to help. I didn't have any training, and I didn't get a job description until much later, so I just followed the leading of Holy Spirit. I made plenty of mistakes; but because I chose to stay in faith, the Holy Spirit always covered me…and He will cover you too.

> **Whatever God has planned for you to become is already inside of you.**

You Have Been Chosen

Here are some basic things that I believe will help, no matter whom you are serving:

You *must* believe that you have been "handpicked" by God. If you didn't know it, I'm telling you now! In God's Kingdom, the way He does things is different from the way the world does them. For example, God promotes based upon faithfulness. You have been selected by your leader to serve them. If you believe that your steps are ordered by the Lord, then you have to believe that He had something to do with it! Of all the people that your leader may know in your congregation, ministry, or organization, they chose *you*. Why do you think that happened? Who do you think told them to choose you? It was *God*, who spoke to the heart of your leader, and said: *"She's the one. I pick her."* And why you? Because God knew in advance that you would be faithful doing it, so He promoted you to the position of serving your leader. In case you didn't know, not everyone has what it takes to serve a leader…but you were chosen because God believes in you! He has commissioned you…and now, with the help of Holy Spirit and this book, He is equipping you to fulfill your responsibility in an even greater way.

It's all part of fulfilling your calling, purpose, and destiny. These are often used interchangeably, but here is how I define them: **Purpose** is *"the reason for which something exists."* You were not born by accident. Even if your birth was unplanned, God still had a purpose for your existence. Jesus came to earth for a purpose.

> *"He that committeth sin is of the devil; for the devil sinneth from the beginning. For this purpose the Son of God was*

manifested, that he might destroy the works of the devil." ***(1 John 3:8 KJV)***

Calling (vocation) is *"God's divine call into His service."* A calling is *"an inward revelation from God of His enlistment of one into outward service."* Many are called, but few are chosen. God may have called you and chosen you to go into the marketplace. God may have called you and chosen you as one of His fivefold ministry gifts. Either way, serving your leader is part of the process of preparing you to serve those in your sphere or the Body of Christ.

"Before I formed thee in the belly I knew thee; and before thou camest forth out of the womb I sanctified thee, and I ordained thee a prophet unto the nations." ***(Jeremiah 1:5 KJV)***

Destiny is where we get the word *destination*. It is *"the journey and fulfillment of God's preordained total plan for a person's life."* ***Psalm 139*** says that every single day of our lives was written in God's book before one day came to be. Serving your leader is an important landmark on your journey. Don't miss it!

"For he knew all about us before we were born and he destined us from the beginning to share the likeness of his Son. This means the Son is the oldest among a vast family of brothers and sisters who will become just like him." ***(Romans 8:29 TPT)***

"And the LORD looked upon him, and said, 'Go in this thy might, and thou shalt save Israel from the hand of the Midianites: have not I sent thee?'" ***(Judges 6:14 KJV)***

To Know Him

A close relationship with God is necessary to discover your purpose, calling, assignments, and destiny. He is the only one that can lead you in the right direction to discover these milestones. He determines your life's route and creates the map for you to follow. At certain intervals in your life, God will give you clues or "mile markers." He realizes that you won't reach your destination right away because it's a process…a journey. He knows that you will need help along the way. You will need help to navigate the rough terrain and withstand the ambushes of robbers along the way. You will need help to find green pastures and still waters so that you can rest when you grow weary from well-doing. You will need the leading of someone that knows every pitfall and can show you the detours to keep from falling in. Only God can lead you in the way you should go. If you learn to hear His voice, follow His leading, be obedient to His instruction, and stay on the path of faith, you will ultimately reach your destination and fulfill your destiny. Serving your leader is just a stop on your way.

> "…but with your own eyes you saw my body being formed. Even before I was born, you had written in your book everything I would do." **(Psalm 139:16 CEV)**

> "Your ears will hear sweet words behind you: 'Go **this** way. There is your path; **this** is how you should go,' whenever you must decide whether to turn to the right or the left." **(Isaiah 30:21 VOICE)**

Our various assignments help us to move along this pathway toward destiny. Assignments are temporary—they change so that we never get too comfortable where we are…but we must always give our best, for as long as we are there. *(Matthew 25:21, Luke 16:10)* Even if your purpose and destiny are unclear, there is no need to be alarmed. No matter what, as a believer, we've all been called to serve, just like we've all been called to share the good news of the gospel.

So here you are in your assignment, on your way to your destiny. You may not know what you have been created to become ultimately, but you *do* have a purpose *today*. It is to serve your leader...and guess what? That, my sister, makes you a *minister*. According to the Webster II Collegiate Dictionary, a minister is *"one who gives service, care, or aid; attend as to wants or necessities."* Isn't that what you do? Your assignment is to make sure that your leader suffers no damage. (*Daniel 6:2*) How do you do that? By making sure that the only thing she has to focus on is what God has called her to do. (*Genesis 39:6, Acts 6:2–4*)

It's More Than a J-O-B

God has entrusted you with the responsibility of caring for His servant leader. This is your assignment. Notice I called it your *assignment*. What is an assignment? An assignment is *"a position of responsibility"* or *"an appointment."* An assignment is *service to mankind*. In other words, you have been handpicked and appointed by God to a position that holds you responsible for taking care of your leader until God reassigns you to do something else.

If you are employed by the person you are serving, you may need to change your perception about what you do. Our society has conditioned people to see the sole purpose for having a job as an opportunity to collect a paycheck. The employee's investment is to do enough to keep from getting fired and keep the checks coming in. God never created us for a *job*. When God placed

Adam in the Garden of Eden, he wasn't given a job, he was given work...he was given an assignment. We were created to *work,* which is what our assignment, serving our leader, is. There is a big difference between a work mindset and a job mindset, which I will try to explain.

A work mindset is powerful. It provides opportunity for entrepreneurship because you can take ownership of what you've been assigned to do. We all know that we tend to take better care of that which personally belongs to us. We take care of our families, our cars, our clothes, etc. With a work mindset, you take care of what has been entrusted to you as though it belonged to you. You don't sit and wait for someone to tell you what to do... you take the initiative. Yes, you see something that needs to be done and do it, but you are also thinking creatively of ways to make things better.

What about that to which God has assigned us? Having a work mindset will cause you to desire to use all of your skills, gifts, and talents for the greater good. It also provides an environment for creativity and potential to come forth. Potential is the hidden ability within you that only comes out when a demand is placed upon it. Too easily, we become creatures of habit. We like our comfort zones, and we like to get in a groove and stay there. *The problem with a groove is that if you stay in it too long, it becomes a rut, which is easy to get into, but hard to get out of.* Let God bring you out of the rut of mediocrity into the realm of creativity!

> **Demand is the force that unleashes potential!**

When you tap into your creativity, you discover gifts, talents, and callings that have been lying dormant because no pressure was ever applied to bring them to the surface. It's like squeezing a catsup bottle. When you squeeze it, whatever is in there will come gushing out! If you never squeeze it, even though it's full, nothing will ever come out. The catsup will remain dormant.

Having a work mindset also holds true if you are one who serves because it's the same mindset of entrepreneurship or ownership. How you view what you do will determine the impact you will make. By giving you this assignment, God has made it so that a demand can be placed on your potential that's been lying dormant. There will be plenty of opportunities for you to be stretched. Instead of lamenting, yield to it. As you do, you will be drawing upon the greatness within that will empower you to become the *incredible woman that God has created you to be!*

Don't Miss the Miracle

You may be new in your position and don't even know how you got it. You may be a nervous wreck because you don't feel capable or even have a clue of what to do. I know what that feels like. When I started, I didn't have a clue either. I remember establishing with the ushers a set place to sit during service on Sunday. I wanted to sit where my first lady could see me so that she knew I was there in the event she needed something. In the very beginning, when she would enter the sanctuary, I would stand up and remain standing until she sat down! Just picture her, walking into an auditorium filled with 2,500 people who watched as I stood when she entered the room and remained standing until she sat down. I wasn't trying to draw attention to myself or to her—it was my way of trying to show her the honor that she deserved. She soon told me that it wasn't necessary for me to stand when she entered a room. Every time I think about it, I think of the *"smh"* (shake my head) emoji. I was just ignorant and didn't know any better. Some things you just have to learn as you go! Thank God for the Holy Spirit...

Maybe you aren't qualified. Well neither was I...but that didn't stop me, and it shouldn't stop you either! Others may not think that you're qualified, but so what? Been there and done that too. Don't you think that God knows you may not be qualified? He didn't choose you for your technical skills. You don't have to prove anything to anyone...not even yourself. God has already approved you.

Take a deep breath...now slowly exhale. Start by believing that God has personally chosen you for such a time as this! God is with you; and therefore, you are up for the challenge. You and God are a majority, and He *won't* let you down. Stay in faith!

Maybe you aren't new to this whole serving thing. You've been in your position for quite some time, and you've got it down to a science...but you have lost your edge and your zeal for what you do. Somewhere along the line, you lost the passion for what you are doing. Don't allow the enemy to disconnect your heart from what God has called you to do. Once you do, your productivity will also disconnect, and you'll find yourself doing just enough to get by. I encourage you to talk to the Father God about it. If you don't get an answer right away, don't abandon ship...wait until you hear. In the meantime, I challenge you to go back and rehearse *how* you received the assignment and *why* you accepted it. You were probably so excited about it that you couldn't wait to get started. You were *fully persuaded* that it was your position otherwise you would not have taken it. Whether you know it or not, God put YOU with your leader. You were handpicked by God for this time. It was a divine set-up!

You might be at the point that you are ready to abandon

your assignment because you are overwhelmed and feel that you can't do it, or you believe that your season has passed. Let me encourage you. Don't be like Gideon and miss the miracle that's right before your eyes. God wants to give you a fresh perspective—that's why you're reading this book. Wait upon the Lord. He will let you know if it's time to move on or if you need to refresh, refocus, and recommit. In the meantime, remain faithful. He knows that you are capable of producing more fruit in your assignment. Don't make your move too soon!

Seek the Lord, and ask Him to reignite the passion that you once had in your heart for what you do. Ask him to fan the flames until the cold embers start to burn again. And if you really believe that your season is up then leave gracefully. Respectfully let your leader know in a timely fashion so they will have ample time to find someone to replace you. Be willing to provide training for your replacement if you can. You can never go wrong serving someone else because every seed sown commands a harvest. **(Genesis 8:22)** Trust the Lord of the Harvest!

> *"I know what I'm doing. I have it all planned out—plans to take care of you, not abandon you; plans to give you the future you hope for."* **(Jeremiah 29:11b MSG)**

> *"Before I formed you in the womb I knew [and] approved of you [as My chosen instrument], and before you were born I separated and set you apart, consecrating you; [and] I appointed you as a prophet to the nations."* **(Jeremiah 1:5 AMPC)**

> *"You saw me before I was born. Every day of my life was recorded in your book. Every moment was laid out before a single day had passed."* **(Psalm 139:16 NLT)**

POINTS TO PONDER

- When God looks at you, He doesn't see the person that you see.
- When you receive a prophetic word, it is God speaking what He knows about you.
- God is entrusting you with the assignment of caring for His servant, your leader.
- Seeing what you do as work instead of a job requires a new mindset.
- God personally chose you for your assignment.
- What is the miracle that is right before your eyes that God doesn't want you to miss about your life or your assignment?

CHAPTER 5

A Divine Assignment

※❦※

"Then came Amalek, and fought with Israel in Rephidim. And Moses said unto Joshua, 'Choose us out men, and go out, fight with Amalek: tomorrow I will stand on the top of the hill with the rod of God in mine hand.' So Joshua did as Moses had said to him, and fought with Amalek: and Moses, Aaron, and Hur went up to the top of the hill. And it came to pass, when Moses held up his hand, that Israel prevailed: and when he let down his hand, Amalek prevailed. But Moses hands were heavy; and they took a stone, and put it under him, and he sat thereon; and Aaron and Hur stayed up his hands, the one on the one side, and the other on the other side; and his hands were steady until the going down of the sun."

(Exodus 17:8-12 KJV)

MOSES had been called by God to lead more than two million Israelites into Canaan. The Israelites were under attack by the Amalekites, and they would have to overcome this opposition before continuing their journey to the land that God promised them. Moses knew their victory was assured, and that God would deliver them as He had done before...*but it would not be automatic.* They would have to band together to defend themselves, and God would be with them. Joshua was assigned to serve Moses as his minister. Moses commanded Joshua, who was also his military leader, to lead an army into battle against the Amalekites. He was to choose some of his best men to go and fight with him.

Joshua did as he was commanded. Moses, his brother Aaron, and Hur, of the tribe of Judah, would go to the top of the hill just above where the battle would take place. Moses took his position of leadership and stood at the top of the hill, just like he did before when he stood at the Red Sea. **(*Exodus 14:16, 21, 27*)** It is the responsibility of the leader to uphold God's righteous purpose before His people, just as Moses held up the rod of God, the symbol of His power, in his hand.

> **For any leader to uphold the righteous purposes of God, they must have a steady hand.**

As Moses held up the rod, Israel fought fearlessly, winning against the enemy. But Moses' hands started getting tired, especially the one that held the rod. The rod was probably made of heavy wood and was at least the length of a man's arm. If Moses used the rod as a walking stick, it could have even been the length of his body. Either way, the rod was getting heavier and heavier, until his hand began to ache and his arm burned.

Can you imagine how hard it must have been for Moses to hold both hands high in the air for an extended time? One hand had nothing in it, but it became heavy due to the weight of the entire arm pulling downward and the exertion of effort to keep it up. The other hand was even heavier because it held the rod in it plus the weight of the arm which was also pulling downward. The extended arms and excess weight of the rod caused his body to become off balance. When he could no longer hold up his arm, he put his hand down to rest; and when he did, the Amalekites began to defeat Israel.

Aaron and Hur weren't on top of the hill just so they could get a better view of the fight; their positioning was strategic.

They were there to partner with Moses in God's overall plan of getting His people to the Promised Land. How? By supporting Moses. They did their part to help Moses oversee and be victorious in this unexpected battle. When Aaron and Hur saw what was happening, they positioned a rock under Moses so he could sit down. Then they got on either side of him and held up his hands! Aaron and Hur took the weight and pressure off Moses, and it was because of their support that he was able to remain steady until the sun went down. Joshua and his men won the battle because Aaron and Hur were in position!

Joshua and his men were victorious against the Amalekites because Moses was able to continue to hold up the rod. God gave Moses the vision and plan, and Joshua executed the plan... but it was Aaron and Hur who provided personal support to Moses. It was their belief in the overall vision and mission that birthed forth their creativity to use the technology available to them at that time...a rock! Aaron, Hur, Joshua, and his men were anointed for the execution of what they were specifically called to do. Without everyone's cooperation in completing their respective assignments, God's plan of getting His people to the Promised Land would have been hindered. (It eventually was, but that's a story for another time!)

Leaders Don't Lead Alone

This account gives us clear confirmation that leaders don't lead alone. God gives them the vision and the plan and then sends people to work alongside them to execute the plan and bring the vision to pass. God gives the vision to the leader who casts the vision to others and then they run with it. It's called *interdependence* or *teamwork*. The purpose of a strong and cohesive team is to steady the leader's hands. God has divinely assigned you to be part of your leader's team to steady her hands.

> "Then the LORD answered me and said, 'Write the vision and engrave it plainly on [clay] tablets So that the one who reads it will run.'" **(Habakkuk 2:2 AMP)**

Remember in the previous chapter, we talked about taking ownership. Why is it significant here? Aaron and Hur could have stood by and watched Moses struggle to keep his tired hands from falling to his side and later blamed Joshua's loss on Moses' failure as a leader. Too many of God's people don't reverence His officers or ministry gifts. Yes, leaders are human, but they are not like us. They have been anointed and appointed by God to do what they do. This wrong attitude on the part of Aaron and Hur would have brought about disastrous results. Joshua and his men would have lost the battle, and over two million people would have died. Instead, Aaron and Hur took ownership of the situation and were able to come up with the solution to Moses' problem. They became *solutionists!*

> **Serving our leaders requires us to walk with them...not just work for them.**

The account also said that Aaron and Hur held up Moses' hands so that they would remain steady until the sun went down.

A Divine Assignment

This is powerful. They stood in position and *didn't move until the assignment was completed*. Can you imagine how uncomfortable this had to have been for them? Their own limbs, feet, and bodies had to have gotten tired too. Did they get hungry? Were they thirsty from the heat? Did they have to go to the bathroom? It had to be extremely uncomfortable for them as they made Moses comfortable, but they didn't consider their own needs. They remained steadfast. They remained committed. They remained focused. They endured. How? Why? *Because they were able to see what Moses saw.* They *walked* with him, not just *worked* for him. They had his heart *(we will discuss this in greater detail in a later chapter)*. They knew that if they allowed Moses' hands to slip even for a second that the entire mission would be in jeopardy. This wasn't about them. It was about more than two million people reaching a common goal! They were doing their part to help Moses get them there. Remember, I mentioned earlier that one of your responsibilities as a handmaiden is to ensure that your leader suffers no damage.

Can you see how important you are to your leader? Never allow yourself to get caught in the trap of shrinking what you do down to the daily routine of it. You must be focused. Not just *be* focused but *stay* focused. Being focused means that you are in tune with your leader. You must be sensitive to her needs. This requires watching, listening, and discerning. Staying focused means not allowing other situations or circumstances to distract you from your mission. Aaron and Hur weren't so focused on the battle that they couldn't see that Moses' arms were getting weary. When they realized what was needed, they sprang into action and remained focused until the mission was accomplished.

You should also expect to make sacrifices. In God's Kingdom, there is always an opportunity to sacrifice. Serving is nothing more than sacrifice. To me, *sacrifice* and *serving* are synonymous. It's putting the needs of others before your own. Jesus is the ultimate model of sacrifice and serving. Many will agree that serving can be inconvenient and uncomfortable…but that's why it's called sacrifice! The upholding of Moses' hands by Aaron and Hur was both inconvenient and uncomfortable; however, their sacrifice and service strengthened Moses' leadership, achieved a battle victory, and brought glory to God!

You are the Aaron and Hur in your leader's life. You are the one whom God has entrusted to hold up both of her hands…the right hand of her family life and the left hand of her ministry or business life. God has called her to stand at the top of the hill with the rod in hand but with all of the demands upon her, eventually her hands and feet will grow weary. God sent you to be the one ready to put a rock under her so she can sit down. He sent you to hold up her hands so that she can continue steadily in her assignment. You are the one sent to assist her, encourage her, pray for her, laugh with her, and cry with her…you are the one she can trust. God has equipped you to do this so that she can do everything that He has charged her with until the sun goes down.

Don't ever forget that your being in her life is giving her victory! It's y-o-u! Not everyone can do what you have been called to do. Your place in her life should not be a position of pride, but one of humility. This holds true for anyone who serves a leader. It doesn't matter whether you are male or female—it's all about having a kingdom perspective of what we have been assigned to do.

God has charged you with an honorable and holy responsibility to uphold the arms of your leader. What you do matters.

Don't ever take serving your leader lightly. It is huge in God's eyes!

> *"For the gifts and the calling of God are irrevocable."* **(Romans 11:29 NKJV)**
>
> *"Each of you should use whatever gift you have received to serve others, as faithful stewards of God's grace in its various forms."* **(1 Peter 4:10 NIV)**
>
> *"For we are God's [own] handiwork (His workmanship), recreated in Christ Jesus, [born anew] that we may do those good works which God predestined (planned beforehand) for us [taking paths which He prepared ahead of time], that we should walk in them [living the good life which He prearranged and made ready for us to live]"* **(Ephesians 2:10 AMPC)**

POINTS TO PONDER

- The Father, Son, and Holy Spirit are a team. God never expects His leaders to lead alone.
- You have been divinely assigned and strategically positioned to be a part of your leader's team.
- Taking ownership requires making an investment.
- Creativity is a byproduct of taking ownership of your assignment.
- To be focused means to be in tune with the needs of your leader. Staying focused means not allowing yourself to become distracted.
- Because of your service to your leader, she *will* be victorious!

CHAPTER 6

No Time for Fear

─◈❧ ❧◈─

"For the thing which I greatly feared is come upon me, and that which I was afraid of is come unto me."

(Job 3:25 KJV)

"What I always feared has happened to me. What I dreaded has come true."

(Job 3:25 NLT)

JOB was a very wealthy man who did everything right…on the surface. The Bible says he was an upright man who feared God and abstained from and shunned evil. It also says that God had built a hedge about Job. But Job had one problem…in his heart, he lived in fear. Job had seven sons and three daughters that liked to party. The sons would take turns hosting parties, and they would invite their sisters to eat and drink with them. Once his children were done partying, Job would get up early in the morning and go to the temple and offer sacrifices for each of them, just in case they had sinned and cursed God in their hearts in the midst of their revelry. Scripture says that Job did this continually…why? In lieu of trusting God, Job had come up with a "Plan B," because he believed in his heart that someday, one of his children would sin and curse God. It's interesting that Job was so concerned about the condition of his children's hearts that he never considered what was hiding in his own…*fear*.

Job prayed because he was afraid for his children…and all of them died. He was also stricken with sickness in his body and lost all his wealth. In all fairness to Job, he was totally unaware of the transaction that had been agreed upon between God and the devil concerning Job's faithfulness. We may not always understand why things are happening to us, but we do have something to say about how we are going to respond to them.

By way of his words, Job declared his expectation; and by way of his repeated actions, he lived in anticipation that something bad would befall his children…*and it did*. It was the spirit of fear operating in Job that caused the hedge that God had built around his life to be breached.

If you have ever read the story of Job, you know that in a moment of self-righteous indignation, Job dared question the justice of God but soon came to understand that it was *his own fear-driven speech*…not *God's justice*…that needed correction. *(Job 6:24, 42:3)* In the end, God restored Job's life exceedingly.

An Unseen Force

Actor Will Smith gave an interesting definition of fear in a sci-fi movie that he and his real-life son, Jaden, starred in together. In a line from the movie, he said to his son, *"The only place that fear can exist is in our thoughts of the future. It is a product of our imagination, causing us to fear things that do not at present and may not ever exist. That is near insanity, Kitai (his son's character). Do not* *misunderstand me…**danger is very real, but fear is a choice.***"

I believe that I can confidently say that there is not a person alive who has not experienced fear at some point in their life. It is an insidious thing; ever lurking, waiting for the opportune moment to strike and derail our faith…because it knows that for the believer, *faith is everything.* That's why I took the most time with this chapter because I have learned from personal experience that when fear is allowed access, like a venomous snake, it will strike quickly and hold on until its poison infiltrates your entire life, including your assignment. What exactly is fear?

Webster's II New College Dictionary offers several definitions for the word fear. There are two that are distinctly different from one another.

- *"an unpleasant, often strong emotion caused by anticipation or awareness of danger."*
- *"a profound reverence and awe, especially toward God."* [ii]

It is believed that there is good fear and bad fear. The Bible does not make this distinction so I'm not going to do it here. For the purpose of this work, we will focus on what the Bible calls *"the spirit of fear,"* which, according to Scripture, comes with torment or punishment **(1 John 4:18)**. What the Bible *is* clear about is ensuring that we understand where fear comes from and how we are to deal with it.

> "Fear not [there is nothing to fear], for I am with you; do not look around you in terror and be dismayed, for I am your God. I will strengthen and harden you to difficulties; yes, I will help you; yes, I will hold you up and retain you with My [victorious] right hand of rightness and justice." **(Isaiah 41:10 AMP)**

The word fear used in this verse is defined in Strong's Concordance (#3372) as the Greek word *Yare'* (yaw-ray) which means *"affright, to make afraid; dreadful, or to fear."* This translation of fear occurs 331 times in the Bible.[iv] It would appear that the Bible has a lot to say about fear and how not to succumb to it!

Second Timothy 1:7 gives clarity as to the source of fear: *"For God hath not given us the spirit of fear; but of power, and of love, and of a sound mind."*

The word *fear* in this verse is used only once and is defined in the Strong's Greek Concordance *(#1167)* as the Greek word *Delia (di-lee-ah)*. Its root is *Deilos (#1169)* which means *"dread; timid, faithless--fearful."* In place of the word fear, other translations of this verse use the words *timid, timidity, cowardly, cowardice, and fearfulness.* This verse also makes it clear that God is not the source of fear. Fear was released into the earth when Adam sinned. According to **Genesis 3**, when Adam realized that he had disobeyed God, he hid from Him. Why? One word…*fear*. When was the last time God asked you to do something, and you hid, or even disobeyed…because of *fear*?

Friend or Foe?

As previously stated, it is believed that there is good fear. If you follow Scripture, fear is not a friend but a formidable foe. Webster's II New College Dictionary defines a foe as *"a personal enemy; a wartime enemy, an opponent, something that opposes, injures and impedes."*[v] The word formidable is defined as *"arousing fear or dread; difficult to overcome, defeat, or overtake."*[vi]

The reason that I consider fear a formidable foe is because it functions stealthily, giving itself the advantage of being able to go undetected. Like a chameleon, it can adapt to any situation.

It lies dormant, waiting for the right opportunity to manifest. Because it is a spirit, fear can't be seen with the natural eye, yet you can see its effects like the wind. It can cause your palms to sweat, knees to knock, heart to race, and sleep to be lost. Fear can disguise itself to the degree that you may think that you aren't operating in it, until something happens that triggers emotions that validate its existence and influence. In other words, *you can pretend like you aren't living in fear, but your speech and actions will reveal the truth.*

God knew that we would face the spirit of fear often so He made sure that we understood its origin, and that we could stand up to it. And that's why He told us *one hundred and forty-four times* in His Word to FEAR NOT, including sixty-three exact phrases between **Genesis 15:1** and **Matthew 10:28** that challenge and encourage us to "fear not."[iii]

This knowledge concerning fear will be valuable to you as you serve your leader because if you haven't already…you will surely face it as you go forth to fulfill your assignment.

Fear thrives on hindering your progress by causing you to believe in an impending threat or danger. It can cause worry, anxiety, procrastination, and even paralysis simply because of the belief that something bad is going to happen without any concrete evidence to support it. You have to learn to identify it and have the determination to push through it.

If allowed, fear can exert so much pressure that it causes you to make wrong or irrational decisions based solely on something imagined. While there are many things that people are afraid of, the four most common fears that seem to plague people are *fear of failure, fear of poverty or lack of provision, fear of death,* and *fear of uncertainty.* We can look at our society today and see how fear is driving people in response to the Covid-19 pandemic. It's interesting that the things that people are worried about seem to fall into these same four categories.

For the believer in Jesus Christ, fear is more than *False Evidence Appearing Real.* It is a spirit that can cause *Failure (to) Exercise Authority (in) Righteousness* against the adversary of our soul. Fear plants the seed of doubt that roots unbelief in God and His Word, ultimately producing a harvest of rebellion. Fear will always appear when you make the decision to trust God. How many times has God told you to give and your mind immediately started listing the reasons why you couldn't or shouldn't? *Doubt... unbelief...rebellion.* Fear wants you to sit on the throne of your own heart; to trust in your own intellectual reasoning, your own self-sufficiency, and rule your own life apart from God.

> **The spirit of fear will cause us to reason ourselves out of God's best for our lives.**

You must resist fear at all costs; because if you tolerate it, your faith will surely be contaminated. Fear is a spirit just as faith is a spirit...but fear is a *perversion* of faith. It has the same capabilities and effects that faith has...except with disastrous results. **Romans 10:17** says, *"So then faith comes by hearing, and hearing by the Word of God."* Fear comes by hearing and believing the word of satan. Even a little fear tolerated is destructive, because it won't be satisfied with just procrastination or paralysis. Fear's agenda is to bring about destruction and even death. Fear is an evil force. It's the magnet that will attract to you the very thing that you fear. What we fear the most will eventually come upon us and have mastery over us. *Just ask Job.*

Oil and Water Don't Mix

There are only two ways to go in life. The way of *faith* or the way of *fear*. They are like oil and water…they don't mix. You can't operate in both—it's either one or the other. Whatever is in the heart will eventually manifest or be played out. The Scriptures say, *"As a man thinks in his heart, so is he." (**Proverbs 23:7 AMPC**)* You will eventually become what you believe in your heart. It's like squeezing that catsup bottle; when pressure is placed on you—what's in you will surely come out. That's why we're seeing such instability in people today. Fear is pressuring people to behave in ways not seen before. Why? People will always move in the direction of their most dominant thought.

You *must* deal with any insecurities, self-esteem, or identity issues; because if you don't, you will be so focused on your deficiencies that you will become double-minded and unstable in your performance. You will either be timid in your delivery of directives from your leader to others for fear of not being accepted, or you will be so arrogant that you will alienate everyone that you come in contact with, all because of your need to prove to others who you think you are. The bottom line is FEAR!

The higher the profile of the one you serve, the more confident and comfortable you must be in your identity. You have to *know who you are, and be okay with it.* Failure to be grounded in this area will hinder your ability to serve effectively which can impede your leader's forward progress. You don't want to become a ball and chain around their ankle instead of the Aaron or Hur holding up their hands. You have to keep it all in perspective and maintain balance.

Always remember the two ends of the spectrum to which you can swing. On one end, you can feel inadequate and intimidated by the responsibility. Though you were chosen for the assignment, you don't feel that you're qualified or worthy. *Never mistake timidity for humility.* They are *not* the same thing. I once read a definition of humility that I have never forgotten. It said, *"Humility isn't not thinking of yourself. It is thinking of yourself **less**."*

Insecurity, lack of confidence, and the like are all fear based. These negative views of yourself cannot be an option. What you do is much too important. If you allow these fears to rule you, they will block the power of God that you need to empower you from flowing through you.

Did you know that your leader can sense fear operating in you? How? Fear will manifest itself in your behavior and in your work performance. Remember what I said previously about the catsup bottle. If not dealt with, your fears will infect your relationship with others, especially your leader. They can become a stumbling block to you and them. You can cause your leader to lose focus and even momentum. Fear operating in your life can become a distraction to you and to them. They need you to help them complete the mission; but once you start embracing your fears, they will make you doubt your ability do the job…and once you *buy the lie*, you will sabotage yourself.

The spirit of fear will also have you overcompensate and overcommit to please your leader and others. You will find yourself making unnecessary mistakes by trying so hard to do everything right. But the more you mess up, the more you will believe you aren't capable. You'll become a *"yes"* person, always agreeing to things you know you can't or don't want to do just to stay in someone's perceived good graces…and then you will really find yourself in over your head!

If any of this resonates with you, I want to encourage you to *quit trying to disqualify yourself*. You don't have to be fearful about your assignment or your ability to perform it. No more walking on *pins and needles* around your leader…and no more *people-pleasing*.

You are co-laboring with your leader to advance God's Kingdom. You can be confident in the fact that *God has called you to this position, and he has equipped you for the task at hand.* If you are a believer, you can do anything through Jesus Christ who is your strengthener! **(*Philippians 4:13*)** You also have help in the form of Holy Spirit. **(*Zechariah 4:6, John 14:26 AMP*)** There is no room or time for fear!

The other end of the spectrum is pride. You may be someone who secretly thinks that you're "all that and a bag of chips" because of who you have been assigned to serve or because "you've got this." Apostle Paul tells us how we should think: *"For by the grace (unmerited favor of God) given to me I warn everyone among you not to estimate and think of himself more highly than he ought [not to have an exaggerated opinion of his own importance], but to rate his ability with sober judgment, each according to the degree of faith apportioned by God to him."* **(*Romans 12:3 AMPC*)**

He didn't say for you not to think *highly of* (overestimate) yourself. He said not to think *more highly*. Pride is thinking more highly of yourself. You must never have an inflated opinion of yourself…especially in your position. What you do and how you treat others is a reflection on your leader before it is a reflection on you. You stand in the place of your leader, ministry, or organization when dealing with others. Whether someone's experience with you is good or bad, they won't tell others how YOU treated them…they will tell them how they were treated by the leader, ministry, or organization. Don't let their reputation become tarnished because of you.

> *"Let nothing be done through strife or vainglory; but in lowliness of mind let each esteem other better than themselves."* **(Philippians 2:3 KJV)**

Out of Balance

We are called to esteem others, not ourselves; and yet somehow, this has gotten out of balance. On one hand, we can stand in line all day long to get an autograph or photo from our favorite actor, singer, author, or sports star; but when it comes to those that God esteems, we oftentimes don't want to honor them, especially when we've allowed ourselves to become too familiar with them. This is not pleasing to God. Failing to esteem others doesn't hurt *them*, it hurts *us*. It's a form of pride, and we only have destruction to look forward to. I know that may sound intense but it is the *truth*! Destruction is synonymous with loss. We lose out when we fail to esteem others. God can use anyone He desires to get to us what He wants us to have or where He wants us to go. We must be willing to humble ourselves, and be obedient to God's instruction.

Recently, God impressed upon my heart to call a young woman that I didn't know very well. We had only met a couple of times at church functions, and it had been some years since I had seen her. I had asked Him for direction, and her name came up in my spirit. My first reaction was that of confusion because I had no history with her. My next reaction was prideful, as I told myself that she was half my age and could not possibly help me. I thank God that I humbled myself and reached out to her, because it was one of the best decisions that I've ever made. She was able to give me insight and help me to work though some things that were causing fear in my own heart. She basically coached me to freedom! Had I allowed pride to stop me from reaching out to her, I would still be struggling with the same issues. Thank God for freedom!

Maintaining balance in how you view your leader is important to serving effectively. Those we serve are *deserving of our honor and respect*; however, we are *not* to put them on a pedestal. They are anointed and appointed…but they are not God Himself; they are His representatives. The danger of putting them on a pedestal is that when (notice I didn't say *if*) they do something that we may deem as "un-pedestal like," then lack of maturity will allow disappointment and even disillusionment to take up residence. This immature response can taint the relationship and become a distraction that will make it extremely difficult to carry out the assignment. We are called to *esteem* our leaders, not *idolize* them. We must respectfully maintain the proper perspective concerning them.

Even in the highest of high-profile positions, IT'S NEVER ABOUT THEM, and it's certainly NOT ABOUT YOU or ME. It's not about "believing your own press" or getting caught up in the hype of who your leader is. It's about God and His purpose being manifested on earth. It's about being focused, staying focused, and handling your business, which is protecting the anointing upon your leader so that God's will can be done. It's

> **Fear is real. DO NOT draw back. Run to it like David did to Goliath, and cut off its head!**

about maintaining your perspective in what you do and whom you serve.

What has been going on in your life that has been causing you to fear, but you've been too afraid to deal with? Has fear been holding you back? Have you been dragging your feet because you know it is time for you to "up your game?" I decree that today is your day! No more procrastination. No more hiding, making excuses, or blaming others. Maybe now is the time to put on your "big girl pants," suck it up, square your shoulders, and get on with your life. Whatever it is…FACE IT! Stand up to your fears. Don't let them bully you! DO NOT draw back. Run to it like David did to Goliath, and cut off its head! God is with you, and He will help you through it.

You may have to make a financial investment in yourself by taking a class to sharpen your skills or purchasing a new wardrobe more fitting to where you want to go. Or possibly, you need to seek out a mentor or coach for personal development, like I did. If you can't do any of these things just yet, be encouraged. It's a process. You can start right where you are by resisting fear and daring to set your sights higher. See who you are and what you do from a bigger and broader point of view. Start looking through the lens of possibility instead of defeat! Did you know that with God, you are a majority, and all things become possible? You can rejoice because serving your leader is not your final destination, but rather a stop on your journey to greatness!

The Bible says, *"The steps of a good man are ordered by the Lord."* **(Psalm 37:23 NIV)** If you believe that the Lord orders your steps, then shake off those negative feelings of inadequacy, timidity, apprehension, and just plain ole fear! Step into your assignment because you have been *anointed and appointed by*

God to do it, and therefore…*you are well able!* There is no fear in love because perfect love drives out fear, which has to do with torment and punishment. God didn't place you in your position to torment or punish you. He put you there to promote you!

> *"Such love has no fear, because perfect love expels all fear. If we are afraid, it is for fear of punishment, and this shows that we have not fully experienced his perfect love."* **(1 John 4:18 NLT)**
>
> *"Jesus said unto him, 'If thou canst believe, all things are possible to him that believeth.'"* **(Mark 9:23 KJV)**
>
> *"I can do all things through Christ that gives me strength."* **(Philippians 4:19 KJV)**

POINTS TO PONDER

- Your mouth will always betray you when fear has taken up residence in your heart.
- One of satan's best tactics is to convince you that you are not capable of completing your assignment.
- Walking in fear blocks the anointing from flowing in your life.
- When you act from a place of fear around your leader, they can sense it.
- Being intimidated or in fear of your leader will cause you to make mistakes.
- Your insecurity will hinder you and impede your leader's forward progress.

CHAPTER 7

Cultivating a Servant's Heart

"Jesus, knowing that the Father had given all things into His hands, and that He had come from God and was going to God, rose from supper and laid aside His garments, took a towel and girded Himself. After that, He poured water into a basin and began to wash the disciples' feet, and to wipe them with the towel with which He was girded. So when He had washed their feet, taken His garments, and sat down again, He said to them, 'Do you know what I have done to you? You call Me Teacher and Lord, and you say well, for so I am. If I then, your Lord and Teacher, have washed your feet, you also ought to wash one another's feet. For I have given you an example, that you should do as I have done to you. Most assuredly, I say to you, a servant is not greater than his master; nor is he who is sent greater than he who sent him. If you know these things, blessed are you if you do them.'"

(John 13:3–5, 12–17 NKJV)

JESUS was in His final hours on earth. His mind was not upon avoiding death, but upon imparting (His) life into His disciples. After eating His last meal with them, He did something extraordinary. He lovingly demonstrated a powerful principle to them (and us.) He got down on His knees and washed their feet! The one who is the express image of God. The one in whom ALL THINGS CONSIST. The very one who created the dust and formed man from it was now washing the feet of His creation. It was Jesus, the same one who would wash the feet of His betrayers without partiality. Jesus knew that one of the disciples would be a co-conspirator in His arrest, conviction, and crucifixion... and yet, He washed his feet. He knew that another one would deny Him three times to the point of cussing His accusers...and He washed his feet too.

Why and how could Jesus do it? He tells us in the Scripture above: *"For I have given you an example, that you should do as I have done to you."* Jesus used the washing of the disciple's feet as a teaching moment. His illustration and demonstration allowed them (and us) to see "up-close and personal" what selflessness looks like. Jesus expected that they would learn the lesson and replicate it. It wasn't the act that He was expecting them to replicate. He was planting the seed that would be cultivated in their hearts to sacrificially serve others, no matter who they were. Jesus knew that the other disciples would eventually learn that Judas betrayed Him, and Peter denied Him. They would also remember that Jesus washed their feet.

What would you do if you were asked to get down on your knees and wash someone's feet? Not just anyone, but someone whose feet were dirty, crusty, and stinky? Could you remove their old worn shoes, and peel off their smelly socks? Could you do it if the person was wearing new socks and shoes? In either case, if the person had never experienced the love of God and this was the only way they could, would you allow yourself to be used to make the introduction? Could you get a basin and towel and get down on your hands and knees and wash their feet? I'm not talking about doing it for a sick child, relative, or spouse. Could you do it for a coworker? Or your boss? How about your leader? What about that one person that you can never seem to get along with?

I would like you to take a moment and think about the questions you just read. Don't just breeze by them. Read the questions again and then ponder them for a moment. As you do, I want you to pay close attention to how your heart is responding. Be honest. Do you find the thought disgusting or demeaning? Do you feel like it's beneath you? Do you find it humbling or humiliating…would you be willing to do it, if asked? Do you find it difficult to even fathom, considering that the times in which we live are so filled with fear and dissention? Whatever you're feeling is probably an indicator of the depth of your heart to serve. *Please do not be offended—I am not judging or criticizing. I'm merely asking as a means to provide opportunity for you to see what's in your heart as it relates to serving others.*

When you became a believer, you forfeited all rights to your life. It is no longer yours. You were appointed as an Ambassador for Christ to represent Him. Your mission is to manifest God's love on earth by serving humanity. No believer is exempt from this; and since you are representing Him, Jesus has the right to set the standard for you to follow. To meet the standard, you must plant the seed of God's Word into your heart so that it can grow into a tree with fruit that will feed nations. **Philippians**

2:5-8 is a powerful seed that you can begin to sow into your heart by way of meditation.

> *"Your attitude should be the kind that was shown us by Jesus Christ, who, though he was God, did not demand and cling to his rights as God, but laid aside his mighty power and glory, taking the disguise of a slave and becoming like men. And he humbled himself even further, going so far as to actually die a criminal's death on a cross."* **(TLB)**

Jesus doesn't expect you to die on a cross…but He *does* expect you to die to self…daily! Jesus was the epitome of selflessness. He set Himself aside to serve others. Oh, what sacrifice! Oh, what love! We must be willing to do the same. Someone sent me a meme recently, and I kept it, because it really ministers to me and helps me to keep things in perspective. It says, *"How do we know if we have a servant's heart? By how we act when we are treated like one!"*

Jesus cared about people. Everything He ever did was for the betterment of people. Again, He spent the last hours of His life caring for His followers…even His betrayers. He esteemed, equipped, and empowered them. And what's so amazing is that *He's still doing it today.* The difference is that He's working through people like you. You're His hands and feet. As His follower, how can you give anything less? Yes, you live in a world that makes it extremely difficult to consider others. *But you are not of this world!* To be part of God's Kingdom and not have a desire to relieve the suffering of humanity is an oxymoron!

God is not asking or expecting you to wash the feet of your leader as part of your service to them. He's just asking you to have the heart of one who would be willing, if He asked you to! *Could* you? *Would* you?

For the Love of Selfie

The Scriptures say that in the last days *"Men will be lovers of their own selves."* **(2 Timothy 3:2)** Another translation says, *"People will be lovers of self and utterly self-centered."* **(AMP)** A third one says, *"For people will only love themselves and their money."* **(NLT)** There are those that mock the Bible as being nothing more than a "dusty old book that has no relevance." But we can see how this belief has affected our society through increased crime rates, racism, and divisiveness in our government.

Due to the pandemic that has plagued our world, social media has become the primary source of communication for the masses. There is a wealth of information that can be obtained and if need be, disseminated quickly. People living in different parts of the world can stay connected. The live streaming of events enables people to join in right where they are. Family members can connect without being in the same location. Social media provides great benefit to our society; but just like anything else, it can and has been misused.

> *"How art thou fallen from heaven, O Lucifer, son of the morning! How art thou cut down to the ground, which didst weaken the nations! For thou hast said in thine heart, '**I will** ascend into heaven, **I will** exalt my throne above the stars of God: **I will** sit also upon the mount of the congregation, in the sides of the north: **I will** ascend above the heights of the clouds; **I will** be like the most High.'"* **(Isaiah 14:12-14, KJV)**

Thousands of years ago, an angel, Lucifer, was expelled from heaven because he had a desire to "be like God." Note the verse above…*five times* he referred to himself. Even though his plan never came to fruition, his *desire* never changed. He has to get people to do what he wants in order to keep his own system going. He influences people to become enamored with themselves. It's like a parent pressuring their child to do something they always wanted to do themselves but missed the opportunity. He's using the many social media platforms to perpetuate the promotion of SELF.

I believe that social media is a powerful tool, especially for commerce and in our time of quarantine and social distancing. Countless millions have been able to hear the gospel preached weekly with the opportunity to give their lives to Christ; however, at the same time satan has made it enticingly easy for people to become enamored with self. You can showcase to the world just how great your life is…it's all about *self*. If you don't like your life, you can make one up,…*it's all about self!* You can make all the "friends" you want to satisfy your sense of loneliness…it's all about *self*. You can get all the "likes" you want to alleviate rejection…it's *still* all about *self!* If you don't like someone's opinion, you can bash it and them…it's *Self! Self!* and more *Self!* Sadly, far too many of God's people have been drawn into satan's intoxicating social media web.

If you are spending more time on social media than you are studying the Word of God and praying, you may need to fast from it. It will be very difficult to have a concern for serving others if you are constantly preoccupied with your own self-promotion.

> *A servant's heart must be cultivated in order for the seed of serving to grow.*

How Does Your Garden Grow?

To cultivate something requires nurturing. The suffix "ing" at the end of the word means *"action"* or *"process."* It's like tending plants in a garden or a home. In the early stages of the plant's growth, you will begin to see small buddings come forth, but that's not the time to stop watering it. You have to continue taking care of it, or it will die. You foster growth through an ongoing process.

Having a servant's heart is *possible*...but not *automatic*. Depending upon the condition of the heart, for some, it may come easy; but for others, not so much. Everything begins as a seed, even a heart to serve. A servant's heart must be cultivated and attended to for the seed of service to grow. It's like growing beautiful flowers in a garden. They all begin as seeds, and the picture on the packet only reveals what the flowers can become if properly cared for. The soil must be prepared and maintained for the plants to grow. The growth process doesn't begin until the seeds are planted. The cultivating of a servant's heart is an ongoing process that begins with having the right attitude.

Most people understand attitude in terms of being either *good* or *bad*. When someone is known to have a bad attitude, everyone avoids them like the plague. When someone is known to have a good attitude, everyone enjoys interacting with them. You have probably heard the saying, *"Your attitude determines your altitude."* Attitude is *"the way we think or feel about someone or something that causes us to behave in a certain way."* This is also known as your *perspective*. Perspective is *your point of view*. It is *"the lens you see the world through and determines how you view yourself, others, and everything else around you."* When you talk about perspective, you have to include perception because *one* is influenced by the *other*.

Perception is *what you interpret*. It's your understanding of a given situation, person, or object. It is the meaning you assign to any given stimulus. Your *perception* is what formulates your *perspective*. Whether right or wrong, *your perception is your reality*. Simply put, your perception is the eyeglass frame that holds the lens of your perspective. (From John Maxwell's *Perception vs. Perspective*)

You can rephrase the above altitude quote and say that *"The way you look and think about things or people or your point of view will determine how far you can go in life."* Because attitude and perspective are synonymous, we will use them interchangeably. The way you look and think about serving your leader will determine how successful you will be at it. Perspective is everything!

It's All About How You See It

You can be a nice person and still have the wrong attitude or perspective apart from the Word of God. It takes more than being a nice person to serve others. It takes having the right attitude, which comes from seeing things from God's point of view. It wasn't Jesus being a "nice person" that got Him through the things He faced. How do you get down on your knees and wash the feet of your betrayer? How do you have the right attitude when you know you are about to die? Jesus was able to do it because He saw everything from God's perspective. In the Garden of Gethsemane, Jesus demonstrated the right attitude because He understood His assignment:

> **Your perspective is formulated by your perception.**

> *"He went on a little farther and bowed with his face to the ground, praying, 'My Father! If it is possible, let this cup of*

suffering be taken away from me. Yet I want your will to be done, not mine.'...Then Jesus left them a second time and prayed, 'My Father! If this cup cannot be taken away unless I drink it, your will be done.'" **(Matthew 26:39, 42 NLT)**

Jesus knew the will of God and understood His purpose in relation to it. He declared in **John 6:38**, "For I came down from heaven, not to do my own will but the will of him that sent me." **(ESV)** If you read the verses after this one, He went on to express God's will in detail. Jesus had the right attitude or *perspective* about His assignment. He understood *(perception)* the will of God, and He aligned himself to it. Having the right perception or understanding of God's will makes cultivating a servant's heart possible. Your *perception* is what formulates your *perspective*. Your lack of understanding and alignment with truth will affect every area of your life including your assignment. If your point of view is wrong about what you've been called by God to do, you won't believe that what you do has a higher purpose. The wrong point of view will have you to devalue what you do, never striving for excellence but instead producing fruit that is mediocre at best.

To reinforce, cultivating a heart to serve begins with having God's perspective. To serve others as Jesus did requires that you operate on a higher level, which manifests greater as you mature in God. You increase in maturity by spending quality time in God's Word and then adopting His mindset as your own. His perspective becomes yours, and you begin to act like Him. You must constantly renew your mind to the ways of God to maintain His perspective.

Having God's perspective will always bring you to a place of humility. Serving like Jesus begins, continues, and ends with humility every step of the way. What is humility? The simplest way to explain it is *"Thinking of others more than you think of yourself."* It doesn't mean that you think of yourself *less*, it just means that you are willing to put others *first*. You are at the point that you are so dependent upon God that you empty yourself to let Him fill you with Himself. He can then operate through you to be a blessing to others.

Also, when you have God's perspective, you place a high value on the anointing that has been placed upon your leader's life. You understand the importance of what they do and how it impacts God's overall plan of expanding His Kingdom. In other words, you are willing to humble yourself under their leadership because you know that what you do will also contribute to God's plan. What *you* do enables them to do what *they* do. When you humble yourself to serve your leader, you are humbling yourself to God. You are doing what Jesus did.

You Are What You Think

Proverbs 23:7 says, *"For as he thinks within himself, so he is."* (***NASB***) Another translation says, *"Be careful how you think; your life is shaped by your thoughts."* (***GNT***) ***Proverbs 4:23*** admonishes us to *"Guard your heart above all else, for it determines the course of your life."* (***NLT***) These Scriptures are letting you know that your life will ultimately follow in the direction of your most dominant thoughts. In other words, your *thought* life determines how you *do* life.

I'm not sure people understand how important their thoughts are. Just because it's in your head doesn't mean that you are the author of the thoughts that you think. You can't afford to allow any thoughts, especially wrong ones about your past, identity, abilities, etc. to roll around in your head like clothes in a dryer.

You have to *manage* your *mind*. Failure to do so can result in a wrong attitude. You have to be intentional about thinking the right thoughts to maintain the right attitude. Having the right attitude is more than deciding to "have a nice day." It's putting away childish things, such as an immature thought life, and aligning your thought life with truth. When you align your thoughts with the Word of God, you will have the right attitude or perspective because you will see your identity and purpose through the lens of truth. Truth never changes; it's not swayed by popular opinion...it doesn't move. It's rock solid. *Truth* is *Truth!* What are some of the things you think about? What thoughts have you allowed to become the highest priority in your mind? What do you think about yourself? What do you think about your leader? Your assignment?

Watch Your Mouth

> *"...For out of the abundance of the heart the mouth speaks."* **(Matthew 12:34b ESV)**
>
> *"It's the same with people. A person full of goodness in his heart produces good things; a person with an evil reservoir in his heart pours out evil things. The heart overflows in the words a person speaks; your words reveal what's within your heart."* **(Luke 6:44–45 VOICE)**

Your words are like the output of a computer. Have you ever heard the term *"garbage in, garbage out?"* If you allow wrong thoughts to be put into your system or "processor," then the output will be the wrong words spoken. Your words guide where you go, what you can have, and what you will become. Your words are the GPS of your life. The words you speak tell what kinds of seeds have been planted in your heart. If you listen to a person long enough, you can tell what kind of seeds or plants they have allowed to grow in their heart. If you don't correct your speech, the plants will ultimately grow into trees that will affect every aspect of your life. Your words carry much more weight than you realize. What have you been saying?

"Death and life are in the power of the tongue: and they that love it shall eat the fruit thereof." **(Proverbs 18:21 KJV)**

"Your very words will be used as evidence against you, and your words will declare you either innocent or guilty." **(Matthew 12:37 TPT)**

You may not realize it, but your life is directed from the inside out, and every seed produces after its own kind. This means that the type of trees that have grown in you will produce a cycle of fruit or corresponding thoughts, beliefs, words, and actions in your life. A negative cycle can only be broken by reprogramming your thoughts with the *Truth*, which is the Word of God. When you reprogram, three main things occur:

- You discover that most of what you believed was a lie.
- Your mind is renewed, and your thoughts are made right.
- Your beliefs are changed, and you are able to bring forth good fruit.

But even with these things occurring, reprogramming is not enough. You must continue to manage your thought life to keep the wrong thoughts out. It's the same as tending a garden to keep the weeds and bugs out. If you don't manage your thoughts, "weeds and bugs" will eventually overtake what's been planted.

You're In the People Business

Jesus understood that serving others was not all spiritual…and it still isn't! It's definitely no "pie in the sky," and that's why you have to have the right attitude about it. Serving is not easy—it's sacrificial. It's never convenient. It's tireless work, and you may find that you are always on call. There are no accolades to be expected for it. Your work is on the front line, ensuring that the one served suffers no damage. It's downright hard work. It's like that battery bunny; you just keep on giving! And yes, there will be times when you will not feel like doing anything for anybody. Again, no condemnation! Having a servant's heart will always draw you back to the right attitude even when you don't feel like it, providing that you are constantly being watered by the Word of God! Jesus was able to look at His betrayers with eyes filled with love and wash their feet, even though they didn't deserve it.

> *Serving isn't easy… it's sacrificial!*

In the people business, there will be those that you encounter who will bring you much joy as you work with or serve them. And there will also be plenty of opportunities to be offended or to offend someone. There will be people that you will encounter that will rub you the wrong way. I call them God's "sandpaper people." Sometimes, He may use *them* to smooth *you* when you may be getting too rough around the edges. You must always be quick to forgive. In God's eyes, there is no degree of offense that can justify unforgiveness. The danger of offense is that it hardens the soil of the heart so that nothing can be planted in it or grow out of it except bitterness. When you experience offense, you must quickly allow Holy Spirit to guide, direct, and correct you.

He can help you to diffuse your emotions, evaluate your reaction, and show you the best way to navigate the situation *God's way*.

When you have the right perspective, it's easier to implement the Holy Spirit's course correction. *(1 John 1:9)* However, when you don't have the right perspective, it's much harder. When you have the wrong thought life, you can only react one way, because that's how you view life. Your reaction will be beyond your control because whatever is planted in your heart will produce an automatic outflow which can impact a lot of people. The Bible admonishes us to *"guard our heart with all diligence." (**Proverbs 4:23**)*

As it relates to your assignment, having God's perspective and a right attitude about it is so very important. You must place a high value upon it. You have to know that what you do is very important to God. You have to see what you do as a calling from God and not just a job. You have to believe that God has equipped you for the task; and therefore, you are well able. You are anointed for it! Always remember that people will see the level of importance that you place on what you do…and *they will respect you for it at that level.*

When people see me with the first lady, they know that I am on assignment, and they should not bother me because my focus is on serving. I've heard it said that I am very serious, and I never smile. Yes, I do. It's just that I am serious about what I do, and I refuse to allow anyone or anything to distract me. I am always nice and cordial, but it's not a time for me to be chatting with others. I'm there to make sure that the first lady "suffers no damage." When I'm serving her, I'm laser-focused on my assignment because it's all about having the right attitude. I value what I do—it's not a game for me. I've been called, anointed, and empowered by God to fulfill my assignment, and I will give Him (and her!) nothing less than my best.

Having the right perspective about your *assignment* begins with having the right perspective about your *identity*. I said it earlier; our perception fuels our perspective. You will never be able to fulfill your assignment effectively apart from the right view of your identity.

> He could have given the assignment to anyone else, but He didn't...because no one else can do what you do.

Never forget that when you have a poor self-image, it affects your perspective and your attitude. Both of these will impact how you interact with others and administer your duties.

Priority Within Purpose

Let us use Jesus as our example. He understood the importance of establishing *priority* within His *purpose*. If you expect to do what you do well, you must establish priority within your purpose also. Serving your leader and others does not exclude your loved ones. It's easy to allow the false glamour or burden of "serving in ministry" to take you away from your family, which is your first ministry. It may not be intentional, but it can happen. Far too many families have been damaged and even destroyed because they were not prioritized. Serving others, your business, and your church are all important to God, but *your family is the most important*. Your first ministry should *always* be to your family. God would never ask you to do something that would cause you to neglect your home. It was nothing for Jesus to slip away to spend quality time with His Father in the place of prayer.

You *must* make sure that your home is taken care of before you go out to save the world. God created the family *before* the five-fold ministry…and it is not necessary for any of us to put our families on the back burner while we serve our leader. If you ask for help, God will provide it. He will use His power on your behalf without you having to do anything to earn His help. That's His grace! This is one way of knowing that God has assigned you to serve your leader; you will always be able to do everything that is required of you. He will even have your family align with your assignment.

Always do your very best to maintain peace in your home. If there is no peace at home, there will be no peace in your heart, and an unsettled heart will hinder your effectiveness. If there is no peace in your home, you won't be able to focus or function at your best in your assignment. Your body may be on post with your leader; but your mind will be at your house, trying to deal with what's causing the unrest. You never want your service to others to cause your family to resent God. You must maintain the right perspective which is the proper priority toward serving others and your family. Remember…family first!

Balance and Boundaries

Serving others demands that we have balance and boundaries in order to be effective. These powerful tools will help us to avoid burnout and abuse. God isn't expecting us to sacrifice to the point of self-destruction, so we must use wisdom in serving. Everyone needs time to rest, refresh, and regroup. We must listen to our bodies (as well as our families) when we are being told that we need to take time off. Jesus regularly took time away to spend time alone with His Father. Most successful leaders take time away from their busy schedules to replenish themselves. There is nothing that says we must prove ourselves to be "super assistants." Burnout is real, and it can happen to anyone. We must use wisdom.

Setting boundaries is also important because they help to protect us from being misused by others. Boundaries will help us to identify and address opportunities where we find ourselves overextended because we have allowed others to take advantage of us. There are those whose primary goal is to take up your time and suck up your energy knowing full well that they don't want help and have no desire to change. We must be discerning and become comfortable with holding others accountable and giving people space where appropriate.

Servant or Volunteer?

Cultivating a servant's heart is especially important if you are not getting a salary for what you are doing. It's during the times of not receiving any compensation or recognition that God watches to see if you will be faithful to what you have committed to do. It is through faithfulness that God brings about promotion. Don't misunderstand; I am *not* saying that getting a salary makes cultivating a heart to serve any less important. God is always watching and always promotes based upon faithfulness, whether there is a check involved or not. A heart that has been cultivated to serve before getting a salary makes it easier for our motives to remain pure and not become contaminated through a paycheck.

Typically, a person not compensated for doing something for another is called a volunteer. I believe that biblically, there is a distinction between volunteering and serving—it's a different mindset. I am not questioning anyone who uses the term "volunteer" to identify people who give their time to help. I'm just highlighting that our perspective will always guide why and how we do what we do. It will anchor us or shift us when times get tough and the pressure is on, and it will surely expose us if we feel inconvenienced for an extended period of time.

Using the Holy Scriptures as the basis for this work, I'd like to examine the difference between volunteering and serving, from my perspective. Outwardly, both can appear to be the same; however, the distinction is in the heart. An individual can perform the same duties but from a different perspective, depending upon how they perceive what they do. They can perform the tasks apart from having a servant's heart and get them done without any real investment; but to serve like Jesus, the heart of the person has to be like His...*All. In!*

Webster's defines a volunteer as *"a person who enters the military or other service of his own free will."*[i] It also means *"to offer or bestow voluntarily, or without solicitation or compulsion."*[ii] This definition of a volunteer implies that one can decide *when, where,* and *how* they want to give of their time. If they don't feel like it, they don't have to do it. And they determine how much or how little time to allot. Going back to the right attitude, I've seen people "volunteer" as a way of escaping their life challenges. They hide behind it until their problems eventually catch up with them or they are so abrasive to others that no one wants to work with them. In both instances, the focus is not on serving others. It's a wrong motive and attitude.

Webster's 1828 Dictionary defines a servant as *"a person who is the subject of a king; a person who voluntarily serves another or acts as his minister; a person employed or used as an instrument in accomplishing God's purposes of mercy or wrath; one who yields obedience to another."*[iii] In other words, a servant is under the authority or rulership of another even though this definition indicates it could be voluntary. In our case as believers, we are under the rulership or lordship of Jesus Christ who is King of Kings and Lord of Lords. **1 Corinthians 7:23** tells us, *"You have been bought and paid for by Christ, so you belong to him—be free now from all these earthly prides and fears."*

As a servant of King Jesus, you willfully relinquish all of your rights. You really have no say as to when, where, and how you will serve Him because you are surrendering your will to His. When you have the right perspective, you understand that you are serving God when you serve others, and He won't forget it. I'm not saying you should serve just to get something from God; but when you are faithful, He will reward you. A sister that attends my church won a brand new 2020 Mercedes Benz that our pastor gave away during the 2019 New Year's Eve service. When her name was called, she was in another area, serving like she always does. Three other names were called before hers, but the people were not in attendance. What a harvest on seed sown through serving others!

> *"God isn't unjust so that he forgets your efforts and the love you have shown for his name's sake when you served and continue to serve God's holy people."* (**Hebrews 6:10 CEB**)
>
> *"For you shall eat [the fruit] of the labor of your hands; happy (blessed, fortunate, enviable) shall you be, and it shall be well with you."* (**Psalm 128:2 AMPC**)

To Serve Is to Love

Love is displayed, not just in word, but also in deed. To *serve* is to *give*. To *give* is to show *love*. *Serving is an act of love!* Serving is loving others enough to set aside self for their welfare. To serve is the greatest gift you have to offer, and the highest privilege you get to share. When you serve others, you allow yourself to be used by God to reveal an aspect of His nature. When you serve others, you give God an opportunity to express Himself. Our world may not seem conducive, but it's definitely ripe for it. You may not feel capable or qualified…but we *all* have the capacity to serve. We can all cultivate a heart to serve by taking on the posture of humility like Jesus. You can do it…and so can I. We were all created in the image and likeness of God. We have it in us to act just like Jesus because He is God, and the Scriptures tell us that God is LOVE…therefore, *we* are love too!

> *"But it shall not be so among you: but whosoever will be great among you, let him be your minister; And whosoever will be chief among you, let him be your servant."* (**Matthew 20:26–27 KJV**)
>
> *"And he sat down, and called the twelve, and saith unto them, 'If any man desire to be first, the same shall be last of all, and servant of all.'"* (**Mark 9:3-5 KJV**)
>
> *"Your attitude should be the kind that was shown us by Jesus Christ, who, though he was God, did not demand and cling to his rights as God, but laid aside his mighty power and glory, taking the disguise of a slave and becoming like men. And he humbled himself even further, going so far as to actually die a criminal's death on a cross."* (**Philippians 2:5–8 TLB**)

POINTS TO PONDER

- Jesus washed the feet of Judas and Peter, despite knowing that they would soon betray Him.
- How difficult would it be for you to wash the feet of someone you don't get along with, a coworker, or someone you don't know?
- To be part of God's Kingdom and not have a desire to relieve the suffering of humanity is an oxymoron!
- Social media can take your focus away from your assignment if you don't discipline yourself.
- Balance and boundaries are necessary to effectively serve.
- Serving is not easy. It's sacrificial.
- What is your perspective when it comes to serving your leader? Serving others?

CHAPTER 8

Cultivating Your Leader's Heart

~~~~~

"Moses said to Joshua, 'Choose some of our men and go out to fight the Amalekites. Tomorrow I will stand on top of the hill with the staff of God in my hands.'"

(Exodus 17:9 NIV)

"So Moses and his assistant Joshua set out, and Moses climbed up the mountain of God."

(Exodus 24:13 NLT)

"When the people saw the cloud standing at the entrance of the tent, they would stand and bow down in front of their own tents. Inside the Tent of Meeting, the LORD would speak to Moses face to face, as one speaks to a friend. Afterward Moses would return to the camp, but the young man who assisted him, Joshua son of Nun, would remain behind in the Tent of Meeting."

(Exodus 33:10–11 NLT)

IN the above Scriptures, we see an evolution in the relationship between Joshua and Moses. This same thing happens in your relationship with your leader. Moses assigned Joshua the task of leading Israel into battle. With great courage, Joshua went into battle and, with God's help, was victorious and accomplished his mission. Your initial interaction with your leader may be to accomplish tasks for them. Do not despise small beginnings because they are your proving times and can lead to bigger and better things.

In the next Scripture, we see that Moses promoted Joshua to be his assistant. History tells us that Moses only took his direction from God, therefore we can safely assume that God gave Moses the "green light" to make Joshua his assistant. On the surface, one may assume that Moses promoted Joshua because of his courage and skill, but it wasn't Joshua's fighting ability that got him promoted. When God selected Moses to lead more than two million people out of captivity, it wasn't because of his leadership, organization, or time management skills. As a matter of fact, Moses tried to back out of his assignment by using *"slowness of speech and tongue"* as his reasons. **(Exodus 4:10)**

When your leader selected you, she didn't base her decision on your technical skills or abilities. God doesn't choose anyone based on their resume. The Scriptures tell us what's important to God in His selection process:

> *"...The LORD does not look at the things people look at. People look at the outward appearance, but the LORD looks at the heart."* **(1 Samuel 16:7b NIV)**

God summoned Moses to meet with Him on Mt. Sinai. Joshua, now Moses' assistant (other Bible translations use the word "minister") traveled with him (which is what assistants do) up the mountain of God. Moses left Joshua behind and went further up the mountain, disappearing into a cloud. Joshua was not permitted to attend the meeting, yet he remained faithful and waited for forty days and forty nights for Moses to return. I wonder what he did to occupy his time? Did he think something had happened to Moses, and he wouldn't be coming back? Was he tempted to leave? He may have been tempted, but we know he didn't leave, Praise God! Joshua didn't leave the mountain because he was *all in!* He *knew* that God was on the mountain. He *knew* that God had called Moses to the mountain. He *knew* that God was speaking to Moses. He *knew* that Moses would return. Therefore…*he remained.*

You Will Be Like Who You Hang With

I remember many years ago, we had a pastor come to speak at our church who was very "down to earth" in his delivery. He told us in his own African American vernacular that *"You gon' be like who you hang with."* I never forgot this statement. It wasn't proper English…but it *was* Scriptural.

> "Do not be so deceived and misled! Evil companionships (communion, associations) corrupt and deprave good manners and morals and character." *(1 Corinthians 15:33 AMPC)*

When Moses came down, there was evidence on his face that God was on the mountain, and that he had been with Him. This cloud represented *the presence of God!* Who can be in the presence of Almighty God and not be changed? Moses was living proof!

> *"Moses didn't realize as he came back down the mountain*

with the tablets that his face glowed from being in the presence of God. Because of this radiance upon his face, Aaron and the people of Israel were afraid to come near him." **(Exodus 34:29-30 TLB)**

"When Moses had finished speaking with them, he put a veil over his face; but whenever he went into the Tabernacle to speak with the Lord, he removed the veil until he came out again; then he would pass on to the people whatever instructions God had given him and the people would see his face aglow. Afterwards he would put the veil on again until he returned to speak with God." **(Exodus 34:33-35 NIV)**

Think about this: when Moses went up into the cloud-covered mountain, Joshua was with him and was touched by some of the same cloud; maybe not to the extent that Moses was, but he was touched nonetheless.

What was happening to Joshua while he was waiting for Moses? Who was he becoming? I believe that during this forty-day period, God was developing in Joshua patience, endurance, faithfulness, and integrity. Joshua was being made ready to lead Israel into the Promised Land. God is eternal, therefore everything with Him is *now*. He had already selected Joshua to replace Moses upon his death. Remember, God has had every single day of our lives written in His book before one day ever came to be. **(Psalm 139)**

God wasn't going to promote Joshua to lead Israel because of his fighting skills. I said in a previous chapter that God's criteria for promotion is faithfulness. Too many of God's people want to be promoted…but they aren't *faithful*. If you look at Joshua's life, you will see that He was faithful to God. It was Joshua and

Caleb who brought back a good report after scouting out the Land of Canaan. They were the only ones with *"another spirit"* who *"followed God fully."* The spirit they had was that of faith. They were "full of faith" or "faithful." They were the only two of an entire generation that would be allowed by God to enter Canaan. Joshua carried *"the same spirit"* of faithfulness into his service to Moses.

Joshua and Moses' relationship changed on that mountain—**Exodus 33:10-11** shows us what happened. There was an intimacy that developed between them. Moses came down from the mountain with laws, commandments, and instructions from God for His people to live by. Something was established in Joshua as he waited for Moses and then watched him execute all that God had commanded. God had given specific instructions for building a tabernacle or "tent" where He would meet with Moses and be closer to His people. The cloud of God would descend upon the tent instead of the mountain. Not everyone was allowed access into the tent. There were also three levels of intimacy established between Moses, Joshua, and God.

- **First**: Moses and Joshua were the only two allowed to go into the tent.
- **Second**: Moses was the only one able to meet God in the tent face-to-face.
- **Finally**: The intimacy between Joshua and God started with Joshua being allowed to go up the mountain with Moses, then grew to the point of Joshua being allowed to remain in the tent even after Moses came out!

What happened? What is the common denominator that made this possible for Joshua? Moses and Joshua had the *same heart*. They were both wholeheartedly following God. As I said earlier, Joshua and Caleb were the only two out of an entire generation of Israelites whom God allowed to receive the land that He had promised them. He saw something in them that the others of their generation didn't have. God would eventually appoint Joshua as Moses' successor to lead the next generation into the Promised Land.

> *"The only exceptions were Caleb (son of Jephunneh the Kenizzite) and Joshua (son of Nun)—for they wholeheartedly followed the Lord and urged the people to go on into the Promised Land."* **(Numbers 32:12 NIV)**
>
> *"After the death of Moses the servant of the LORD, it came to pass that the LORD spoke to Joshua the son of Nun, Moses' assistant, saying, 'Moses my servant is dead. Now therefore, arise, go over this Jordan, you and all this people, to the land which I am giving to them—the children of Israel.'"* **(Joshua 1:1–2 NKJV)**

Time Well Spent

The more time you spend with your leader, the more you will get to know her. Just as Moses and Joshua spent time on the mountain and in the "tent" together, you will begin to develop her heart as you spend that intimate time with her. You will come to understand what's important to her both in her private life and public ministry. Quite naturally, her husband and family are important; but you will learn about her as a person. You must pay close attention because these are the things that will help you to serve her better. If you don't have one, you need to develop your prayer life because some things that you learn will become prayer projects for you.

Let me take this opportunity to share something very valuable that I learned from my mentor. If someone brings you into a circle or environment where there are people at a higher level than you, it is best to be quiet and b-r-e-a-t-h-e! *This is not the time to be talking.* It's a time to breathe so your lungs can mature. *You should never give your opinion unless you are asked for it.*

As you work for her and with her, you will find yourself participating in various activities that will be personal, ministry, and/or business-related.

During intimate times with your leader is not a time for you to try to impress. It's a time for you to watch, learn, and do, so that you can be impressed with her heart.

During these interactions, you will quickly learn her temperament. You'll find out what she likes and dislikes. You will come to know what she's passionate about, what makes her laugh and brings her joy, what makes her angry and upset, and even how she likes to relax and have fun. You'll learn what she likes to wear, where she shops, her eating habits, and other routines. You will come to know the "whole" woman and not see her as a title or position. You will learn her rhythm and her flow. You will see and adapt to her work ethic. You will see her strengths and her weaknesses. You will see her victories and her challenges. You will learn to recognize her spiritual heartbeat! Any time spent with her is an opportunity to learn more, and you should never take these times for granted. During these times, you should be slow to speak and quick to listen. Pay as much attention to things that *aren't* said as you do to things that *are*.

Au Naturel

You will have plenty of opportunities to see your leader in her natural habitat. You will be interacting with her when the anointing is not flowing. Be mature enough to separate the person from the anointing. We all have good and not-so-good days. Remember that leaders are people too! Your leader has hormones just like you do. If you find that your leader's communication or behavior is challenging in some areas, keep your mouth shut, and take it to God in prayer! Whatever you do, DO NOT let satan get you offended. You must learn to develop a thick skin and not take things personally!

If you feel that you are being mistreated by your leader, you need to take it before the Lord and make sure that you're not being overly sensitive. If, after you've spent time in earnest prayer, you still have an issue, then you have to decide if you should stay in the position. Before you leave, you need to make sure that God is releasing you. The right thing to do is to talk with your leader about it. They may not even be aware that they are doing things that are making you uncomfortable. You need to be *absolutely certain* before you walk away from your assignment!

In the beginning, we are always so very confident that God called us; but when things start getting a little tense or not going the way we think they should, how quickly we forget the call. God is not *wishy-washy* or *double-minded,* and He doesn't change His mind like we do. Ask God…it may be that your leader sees more in you and knows what you are capable of, and is placing a *demand on your potential* so that the greatness in you can spring forth!

Clarity Is the Key

If you don't understand something, say so. *Always* be willing to ask questions, or ask for help. It is a trick of the devil to make you too afraid or prideful to admit that you don't understand an instruction or directive. It can sometimes cost more to make a mistake and then have to go back and make corrections than to ask for clarification up front. Always be prepared to write things down. Create a file or notebook where you can put important information for future reference. It should be more of an exception than a rule that instructions are repeated more than once. Even in Scripture, God encourages us to come to Him when we lack wisdom, and He will give it to us. We are also admonished *"in all of our getting, get understanding."*

It's All About Timing

Even as you learn the ways of your leader, there will still be some things that you will only know by way of discernment. For example, regarding the leader that I serve, there are times when people may come to me for clarity or guidance on a directive she has given, or I may need her approval, direction, or a decision. While there may be a deadline pending, I have come to know and understand that she will not allow anyone to put pressure on her to respond. I have to discern the best time to either present the issue, remind her about it, or just back off. It's all about timing. Before I understood this, I would feel the pressure from others, and I would then put pressure on myself because of a deadline.

One day, Holy Spirit spoke to my heart and told me to trust Him with the timing. He also gave me a way to respond to people who tried to pressure me for an answer. It's found in

Exodus 40:36 which says, *"Whenever the cloud lifted and moved, the people of Israel journeyed onward, following it. But if the cloud stayed, they stayed until it moved." **(TLB)*** In other words, when she made a decision, we would move forward; but until she did, we wouldn't do anything. I decided to do just that; and from then on, He honored His Word. Holy Spirit lets me know when to present something, when to remind her of something, and when to back off. To this day, sometimes I follow these steps and nothing happens—but it's okay because Holy Spirit always lets me know what to do and when. It always gets done. Holy Spirit is my Helper…and yours too *if you ask Him*!

Represent Well!

In your role as her assistant, she and others will see you as her representative and you will have many opportunities to speak on her behalf. You will be her "go-to person" when people need something from her and she's not available, and You have to *know her position and her heart* on certain things. Knowing where she stands *does not* mean that you should arbitrarily make decisions or speak for her. *Don't* assume. Always inform her, when appropriate, and give her the opportunity to decide how to proceed. It's possible that she may have changed her position, and you have not been updated.

Don't be offended if people aren't interested in your opinion—they want to know *hers!* And that's *okay*, especially if you have the same heart that she does. You have to know her position on things to be effective in this area.

I touched on this in a previous chapter, but I believe it's worth reinforcing, especially for those of you who may be the first person encountered in a ministry or business i.e. assistant, receptionist, usher, armor-bearer, assistant pastor, etc. How you interact with others is always a reflection on your leader, ministry, or organization. Whether the interaction is good or bad, the person who had the experience with you won't tell others how YOU treated them. They will tell others how they were treated by the leader, ministry, or organization. Remember...*people will form their opinion about your leader, ministry, or organization based on their interaction with you!*

Jesus never had bad days, and you don't get to have them either. It is not your name, business, ministry, or reputation that is on the line; therefore, you are obligated to treat everyone you come into contact with as their representative with dignity and respect. How you treat people will determine whether or not they ever interact with your leader, ministry, or organization again. REPRESENT THEM WELL!

Can You See What She Sees?

Vision and *commitment* are the two lenses that you need to look through in order to cultivate your leader's heart. Understanding the vision and mission of the church or ministry (or business) is vital. The vision and mission are the compass that guides your leader and the organization and should always be in your focus. You need to understand where she is going in order to help her to get there. If you don't know the vision and mission, you need to find it and put it someplace where you can see it. If you don't have an office or a permanent location to work from, put it someplace where you can see it and have access to it, until you have a clear understanding of it. If the vision and mission aren't too long, try committing them to memory.

It's not enough to just *know* and *remember* the vision and mission…you also have to be *committed* to it. Did you know that you can be involved in something and not be committed to it? How many couples do you know who are living together but won't get married because one or both of them are afraid of commitment? In order to serve someone in the capacity in which we do, you have to understand where they are going and be *all in* to help them get there. You are being allowed into someone's personal and professional lives, and they have to be able to trust your commitment to them…and to their vision and mission…*completely*.

You must have a clear understanding of your role and how it connects to the vision and mission. You have to adopt a global mindset. You have to be able to see beyond the day-to-day affairs of life. You have to become skilled at keeping your eyes on what matters most, no matter what, especially during seasons when your progress seems slow. To serve others requires that you understand both your purpose and the purpose of your leader to the fullest extent. If your leader is a first lady, she is also the pastor's wife, and she supports him in the vision that God has given to him. *Her* vision should complement *his* vision. Their visions are intertwined…therefore, when you get behind *her*, you also get behind *him*. This holds true even if your leader is not the first lady, but the pastor.

Be Nice!

You may be in a church where the culture does not equally esteem the first lady with her husband. If you are in this type of environment, you may encounter those who will try to undermine her with the "Pastor said…" rhetoric. Understanding her level of authority will help you to determine yours. You may even find yourself in the position of being the only ally that she has. Be prepared by being prayed up! When faced with that type of situation, you will need to learn diplomacy and wisdom. Having these tools in your toolbox will help you when interacting with others in politically-charged environments.

Remember, you represent the leader you are serving. You represent the management. People may not like you because of it, but don't let it get next to you. Don't take it personally. Endeavor to treat everyone the same because *the way that you treat people reflects on your leader.* If you are the first encounter that someone has with your ministry or organization and it doesn't go well, like I said before, they won't bash your name, they will bash your leader's name. Don't allow your leader's name to be tarnished because of your nastiness. *Be nice*!

Remember when I talked about the spectrum in an earlier chapter? You don't want to come across as arrogant. You don't want to alienate those you have to work with because at the end of the day, you may need their support to get your job done. Remember…you *represent* your leader, but you are *not* the leader. When it comes to members of your church, the first lady and the pastor are still responsible for the care of God's sheep; therefore, be aware of how you treat them. If you are in a business setting, the same holds true with your customers, clients, etc.

Staying Under Authority

Beware of a haughty spirit. Stay within your boundaries of authority. While you may *know* how your leader may feel on a particular matter, *you still have the responsibility to present it to her, and allow her the opportunity to decide.* I've heard many stories about assistants who didn't return calls or respond to emails; and when asked to have their boss consider an invitation, they declined it without even giving them the opportunity to decide. The assistant arbitrarily decided for them. How do you do that? At this point, you've become *too familiar with the anointing*. This is not wise.

"But when she came to Elisha at the mountain she fell to the ground before him and caught hold of his feet. Gehazi began to push her away, but the prophet said, 'Leave her alone; something is deeply troubling her and the Lord hasn't told me what it is.'" **(2 Kings 4:27 TLB)**

In this story, a prominent woman's son became ill and died while he was out in the fields with his father. Instead of preparing for her son's funeral, his mother laid him in a room in her home that she had built for Elisha, the prophet of God, who had prophesied the supernatural birth of this same son while she was barren, and her husband was old. Believing that the prophet was the only one who could resurrect her son, she saddled a donkey and took off after him.

As the woman approached in the distance, Elisha sent his servant (assistant), Gehazi, to meet the woman to find out if she and her family were well. She answered him, *"It is well."* She didn't waste time telling Gehazi her problem; she only wanted to talk to the man of God. Don't take it personally when people tell you that they would rather speak to the first lady or the pastor instead of you. Remember, they are the shepherds, not you. If neither of them are available, you should try and assist the person by referring them to someone who can help; but if they refuse, don't push. Follow the proper protocol and remember…*be nice!*

When the woman reached Elisha, she fell to the ground and grabbed hold of his feet. When she did that, the servant Gehazi started toward her to PUSH HER AWAY! The prophet rebuked him and told him to leave the woman alone because he could see that something was troubling her. He acknowledged that God had not shown him what was going on with her, so he was trying to find out.

What caused Gehazi's reaction? Why did he try to stop the woman? Was he concerned for the prophet's safety? This woman was not a stranger to them nor would she do the prophet any harm. Gehazi was aware of the relationship between the prophet, the woman, and her husband. He knew that it was because of their generosity that he and the prophet had a place to rest when they came to town. They had built them a room in their home. How much closer could they get? Not only that, but the prophet spoke, and this couple conceived a son supernaturally. When the woman approached the prophet and fell at his feet, it was obvious that something was wrong. So why did he treat her the way he did? He had become *too familiar with the anointing.*

Elisha had served the prophet Elijah for many, many years. He was known as the one who "washed the hands of Elijah." When Elijah was taken to heaven, Elisha received his mantle because he had served him faithfully. In the same spirit, Elisha selected Gehazi from the young prophets that were part of Elisha's school to be his servant. Initially, Gehazi's heart was aligned with the prophets. When Elisha was trying to find a way to bless the woman for her generosity, it was Gehazi's understanding of their state that revealed that the woman and her husband had no heir because she was barren, and he was old. Something had to happen to cause Gehazi's heart to change. When the woman came to Elisha for help, Gehazi was not moved by the woman's distress. He had lost his compassion. He had taken on an attitude of *"I'm Elisha's servant. Nobody is closer or knows him better than I do; therefore, I will decide who gets close to him."* Gehazi had lost the heart of ministry...He had lost the heart of his leader, Elisha, and He completely disregarded the anointing that God had placed upon the prophet to minister to the hurting. Elisha was an oracle of God and not a celebrity in need of protection. (See **2 Kings 6**.)

Things are constantly changing, so the way that your leader viewed something in the past could be completely different in the present. I mentioned this in an earlier chapter—you *must* give them the chance to decide if they want to change their viewpoint. When you get to a place of thinking that you know your leader better than anyone else, others' opinions, gifts, and talents don't matter because "you've been around longer," or "you have to protect them, and no one can do it better," then you have become *too familiar with the anointing.* You have now elevated yourself to an unsafe place, and you risk losing your anointing. Thinking that you know the person so well will cause you to usurp their authority and deny them the right to make a decision or change their mind. When you are in this place, you are no longer operating from the same heart as your leader, but from a place of presumption based upon your assumptions. We all know what happens when we assume. You end up being rebuked like Gehazi!

Learning to separate your daily workings with your leader from the anointing upon their lives is a must. This will facilitate the level of honor and respect due them. I can't say it enough. *You must never become too familiar.* To do so will deny you the benefit of the anointing upon their lives.

When we honor our leaders, are committed to their vision, focused on learning all we can from them to better serve them, and diligent in our execution, something supernatural happens… God gives us the same heartbeat as our leaders.

> "Then Jonathan made a covenant with David because he loved him as himself." (**1 Samuel 18:3 AMP**)

> "But Ruth said, 'Do not urge me to leave you or to turn back from following you; for where you go, I will go, and where you lodge, I will lodge. Your people will be my people, and your God, my God.'" (**Ruth 1:16 AMP**)

> "Two are better than one because they have a more satisfying return for their labor." (**Ecclesiastes 4:9 AMP**)

POINTS TO PONDER

- Your initial interaction with your leader may be task-oriented. Do not despise small beginnings.
- If someone brings you into a circle or environment where there are people at a higher level than you, it is best to be quiet and "breathe."
- If you don't have one, you need to develop your prayer life, because some things that you learn about your leader will become prayer projects for you.
- Assuming you know something when you don't is a form of pride. Always be willing to ask questions or ask for help.
- Do you know and understand the mission and vision of your leader and their organization?
- Becoming too familiar with the anointing upon your leader's life will cause you to lose respect for it.

The Handmaiden's Prayer

Heavenly Father,

I thank you that you have chosen me as one of your handmaidens. I accept this as a holy calling and commit to serve those in leadership to the best of my ability with the help of Holy Spirit.

I pray that the eyes of my understanding be enlightened so that through my knowledge of you, I am confident in who I am in you and will never allow my value to be questioned because I've been chosen to serve others.

I pray that you give me the heart of Jesus so that I can lay aside my own agenda to serve my leader and others without the fear of missing my own destiny.

I thank you that I am able to serve others unselfishly, expecting nothing from them in return and knowing that my reward will come from you because you are not unrighteous to forget my labor of love.

Help me to remain humble and not become weary in doing good, trusting that you will exalt me in due season if I don't faint.

In Jesus' Name. Amen.

Special Thanks!

A special "shout-out" to the sisters who saw in me what I sometimes wasn't able to see myself!

BJ...Mom, everyone knows that I'm your daughter, and you're my biggest fan!

VBW...Thank you for setting such a godly example. You are the reason I'm able to write this book.

Djuana D...Thank you for so freely sharing and imparting your writing wisdom. The baby is born!

Monica M...Thank you for being the prophetic voice in my life!

Marsha C...Thank you for always seeing the best in me!

Renee L...Thank you for not letting me stay in the cave!

Dr. Deloris T...Thank you for your commitment even before seeing the finished product!

Prophetess Kimberly M...Thank you for mentoring me from afar. I have learned so much from you.

Tiffany J...Thank you for confirming the scribe's anointing.

Tammy S...Thank you for being my prayer partner and consistent supporter.

Tasha A...Thank you for giving me the idea to write three books instead of one.

Ashley W... *Thank you for coming into my life at a critical time!*

Sandra C... *Thank you for trusting me to write the foreword to your first book. I'm staying real and free!*

Latasha B... *Thank you for always being willing to help me!*

Pastor (Coach) Kisia Coleman... *Thank you for allowing me to write for you and for sharing your platform. You have helped me to move from writer to author!*

To my daughter, **QUIANA**, and my granddaughters, **TATIANA** and **BRIANA**.
THIS ONE IS FOR YOU!

Thank You, Jesus!

About the Book

Many are called, but few are chosen.

Throughout history, women have served other women. In ancient times, they were called handmaidens. God has chosen and assigned certain women to positions of leadership. He has also handpicked certain women that He commissions to come alongside and undergird these women leaders to help them fulfill their assignments. To be chosen by God to serve another is a holy calling. To be chosen by God to serve another woman is not just a unique opportunity, but a divine assignment.

The Handmaiden's Handbook, Volume One is a guide for women who have been "handpicked" by God to serve women leaders. Whether you're new and have been learning as you go or you've served others and are seasoned, this handbook will be beneficial to you. Written from a biblical perspective, *The Handmaiden's Handbook, Volume One* is designed to lay a strong foundation in your life of serving by offering spiritual insight into this divine assignment. Through biblical truths, you will learn how to offer undeniable, unforgettable service to those who lead. It will inspire you to have a greater heart to serve, and invoke the spirit of excellence while serving.

Whether the woman you serve is a leader in the church or the marketplace, every woman in leadership deserves to be served from a position of honor and with a heart of humility. Let *The*

Handmaiden's Handbook, Volume One inspire and empower you to bring forth a higher level of service because when YOU go up…SHE goes up! And when she goes higher…You go higher!

Finally…after reading this book, don't get bent out of shape if people continue to address you as an "armor-bearer." What they call you is not important. What *is* important is that you have embraced what has been shared in this book, and that you have purposed in your heart to serve your leader with the heart of *God's Handmaiden*.

Endnotes

CHAPTER 1

i 1828 Edition of Noah Webster's American Dictionary of the English Language online s.v. "handmaid," accessed November 1, 2018 http://1828.mshaffer.com/d/search/word,handmaid

ii 1828 Edition of Noah Webster's American Dictionary of the English Language online s.v. "armor-bearer," accessed November 1, 2018 http://1828.mshaffer.com/d/search/word,armorbearer

iii Dictionary.com. Dictionary.com online, s.v. "armor-bearer," accessed November 1, 2018 https://www.dictionary.com/browse/armorbearer

iv Dictionary.com. Dictionary.com online, s.v. "lady-in-waiting," https://www.dictionary.com/browse/lady-in-waiting?s=t
https://www.elizabethan-era.org.uk/lady-in-wait-ing.htm
www.en.wikipedia.org/wiki/Lady-in-waiting
www.cheatsheet.com/culture/surprising-duties-of-royal-family-ladies-inwaiting.html/

CHAPTER 2

i   "Father." Greek translation for "life source," accessed November 1, 2018, Thayer's Greek Lexicon, Strong's NT, 3962, https://biblehub.com/greek/3962.htm

CHAPTER 3

©1996-2019

i   https://www.womeninworldhistory.com>lesson 10

ii   https://www.history.com/topics/womens-history/the-fight-for-women-suffrage

iii   Women's Rights Movement https://www.britannica.com/event/womens-movement

iv   https://en.m.wikipedia.org/wiki/Tarana_Burke

v   https://www.metoomvmt.org/about/#history

CHAPTER 4

i   Dictionary.com. Dictionary.com online, s.v. "minister," accessed March 31, 2020 https://www.dictionary.com/browse/minister

CHAPTER 6

i   IMDb After Earth (2013) – Quotes - IMDb Christopher Raige http://www.imdb.com/title/tt1815862/quotes?qy=qt1946994

ii   "Fear" Hebrew translation for "affright, to fear," accessed February 24, 2020, Thayer's Hebrew Lexicon, Strong's OT, 3372

https://biblehub.com/hebrew/3372.htm
"Foe." Webster's II New College Dictionary. (Boston, MA: Houghton Mifflin Company, 2001, 1999, 1995).
"Formidable." Webster's II New College Dictionary. (Boston, MA: Houghton Mifflin Company, 2001, 1999, 1995).

CHAPTER 7

[i] 1828 Edition of Noah Webster's American Dictionary of the English Language online s.v. "volunteer," accessed November 1, 2018 http://1828.mshaffer.com/d/search/word,volunteer

[ii] Ibid.

[iii] 1828 Edition of Noah Webster's American Dictionary of the English Language online s.v. 5 "servant," accessed November 1, 2018 http://1828.mshaffer.com/d/search/word,servant

About the Author

Denise M. Carlie is the Executive Personal Assistant to the first lady of a global multicultural ministry located in Forest Park, Illinois. She has also served for many years under the first lady's leadership as the Director of the Women's Ministry. Denise is a licensed minister, dynamic Bible teacher, and intercessor. She has a heart to serve and help God's people become strong in their faith so that they fulfill the plan that God has ordained for their lives as mature sons and daughters of God. Her desire is to be remembered as "a woman after God's own heart."

Contact the Author

If you would like to contact the author, you may do so at denisemcarlie@gmail.com

www.ingramcontent.com/pod-product-compliance
Lightning Source LLC
Chambersburg PA
CBHW071404290426
44108CB00014B/1677

Щенок, ручка и игрушка: